D1083625

The Political Economy of Participatory Economics

The Political Economy of Participatory Economics

Michael Albert
Robin Hahnel

Princeton University Press
Princeton, New Jersey

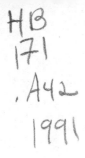

Copyright © 1991 by Princeton University Press
Published by Princeton University Press,
41 William Street, Princeton, New Jersey 08540
In the United Kingdom: Princeton University Press, Oxford

Library of Congress Cataloging-in-Publication Data

Albert, Michael
The political economy of participatory economics / Michael Albert and
Robin Hahnel.
p. cm.
ISBN 0-691-04274-8 (alk. paper)
ISBN 0-691-00384-x (pbk.: alk paper)
1. Economics. 2. Central Planning. I. Hahnel, Robin. II. Title.
HX73.A425 1991
335—dc20   90-23193
                                                  CIP

This book has been composed in Times Roman

Princeton University Press Books are printed on acid-free paper, and meet the
guidelines for permanence and durability of the Committee on Production
Guidelines for Book Longevity of the Council of Library Resources

Printed in the United States of America
by Princeton University Press, Princeton, New Jersey

10 9 8 7 6 5 4 3 2 1

10 9 8 7 6 5 4 3 2 1 (Pbk.)

Contents

I would like to believe that people have an instinct for freedom, that they really want to control their own affairs. They don't want to be pushed around, ordered, oppressed, etc., and they want a chance to do things that make sense, like constructive work in a way that they control, or maybe control together with others. I don't know any way to prove this. It's really a hope about what human beings are like—a hope that if social structures change sufficiently, those aspects of human nature will be realized.

—Noam Chomsky

[We seek] a condition of society in which there should be neither rich nor poor, neither master nor master's man, neither idle nor overworked, neither brain-sick brain workers, nor heartsick hand workers, in a word, in which all would be living in equality of condition and would manage their affairs unwastefully, and with the full consciousness that harm to one would mean harm to all—the realization at last of the meaning of the word commonwealth.

—William Morris

I wish that every human life might be pure transparent freedom.
—Simone de Beauvoir

The Political Economy of Participatory Economics

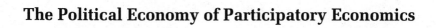

INTRODUCTION

*[We seek] a condition of society in which there should be
neither rich nor poor, neither master nor master's man, neither
idle nor overworked, neither brain-sick brain workers, nor
heartsick hand workers, in a word, in which all would be living
in equality of condition and would manage their affairs
unwastefully, and with the full consciousness that harm to one
would mean harm to all—the realization at last of the meaning
of the word commonwealth.*

—William Morris

The fall of communism confirms century-old libertarian claims
that equity and justice cannot be imposed by force, that interpreting "to each according to work" as "to each according to the
marginal revenue product of one's labor" rationalizes privilege, and
that central planning stifles workers' creative potentials. Clearly,
enterprises whose inputs and outputs have been determined by a
central planning procedure exclude workers and consumers from
decision making, separate conceptual and manual tasks, and offer
unequal consumption and work opportunities. For the Soviet, East
German, Polish, Czechoslovakian, and Hungarian people to reject
these injustices is encouraging. But it is dishonest to say this
demonstrates that capitalism is optimal. It only bespeaks a lack of
alternatives.

In this book we argue for a new alternative based on public ownership and a decentralized planning procedure in which workers and consumers propose and revise their own activities until an equitable, efficient plan is reached. The vision, which we call a participatory economy, strives for equitable consumption and work which integrate conceptual and manual labor so that no participants can skew outcomes in their favor, so that self-motivation plays a growing role as workers manage their own activities, and so that peer pressure and peer esteem provide powerful incentives once excelling and malingering rebound to the advantage and disadvantage of one's work mates.

Heretofore, most professional economists have accepted that human nature and modern technology *rule out* egalitarian, participatory options. They have generally claimed that efficient production must be hierarchical, that effective incentives require inegalitarian consumption, and that allocation can be carried out either by markets or central planning, but not via some alternative "participatory" approach. The following chapters challenge this professional consensus by presenting a plausible, efficient, participatory, egalitarian economic model.

In chapter 1 we review our understanding of traditional economic institutions and practices—markets, central planning, private ownership of the means of production, hierarchical production relations, and inegalitarian consumption—showing how each subverts efficiency, equity, self-management, solidarity, and/or variety.

In chapters 2, 3, and 4 we present a comprehensive description of exactly how participatory production, consumption, and allocation could facilitate economic democracy and justice. In chapter 2 we describe a participatory organization of production and address whether this entails a sacrifice in efficiency. In chapter 3 we describe a participatory organization of consumption and examine whether this implies a dearth of necessary incentives or a loss of individual freedoms. In chapter 4 we describe a participatory allocation system and explain how it reinforces the democratic, egalitarian properties of workers' and consumers' councils.

In chapter 5 we construct a formal model of participatory planning and use it to carry out a welfare theoretic analysis in terms comparable to welfare analyses of traditional models. We determine under what conditions participatory planning can generate Pareto optimal outcomes as well as whether its procedures are incentive compatible. We evaluate likely discrepancies between realistic versions of our economy and its formal model, as well as realistic versions of traditional economies and their formal models.

In chapter 6 we suggest computer simulations and social experiments that could substantiate the feasibility of participatory economics. A concluding postscript summarizes where the debate over alternative economic models stands.

Finally, we should add that readers interested in a more detailed discussion of the newly envisioned relations of participatory economics should consult the companion volume, *Looking Forward: Participatory Economics for the Twenty First Century* (Boston: South End Press, 1991).

1

TRADITIONAL ECONOMIES

Concepts which have proved useful for ordering things easily assume so great an authority over us, that we forget their terrestrial origin and accept them as unalterable facts. They then become labeled as 'conceptual necessities,' 'apriori solutions,' etc. The road of scientific progress is frequently blocked for long periods by such errors. It is therefore not just an idle game to exercise our ability to analyze familiar concepts, and to demonstrate the conditions on which this justification of their usefulness depend.

—*Albert Einstein*

We seek an economy that distributes the duties and benefits of social labor fairly; that involves members in decision making in proportion to the degree they are affected by outcomes; that develops human potentials for creativity, cooperation, and empathy; and that utilizes human and natural resources efficiently in the world we really inhabit—an ecological world filled with complicated mixtures of public and private effects. In short, we want an equitable, efficient, economy that promotes self-management, solidarity, and variety under real world conditions.

Traditional efforts to model a desirable economy often start from views of human potentials we find simplistic, assumptions we find unrealistic, and values we find logically and morally flawed. Nonetheless, to sensibly model a desirable economy, we still need to determine whether, under reasonable assumptions, traditional economic models can accomplish the goals we seek.

Valuative Criteria

First, we accept the traditional view that a desirable economy should be equitable. However, we distinguish four mutually exclusive distributive maxims that different schools of thought have used to define the meaning of "equitable":

1. Payment according to personal contribution and the contribution of property owned.

2. Payment according to personal contribution.

3. Payment according to effort.

4. Payment according to need.

In chapter 3 we debate the relative merits of these competing maxims. In contrast to most traditional economists who opt for maxim 1 or 2, we find that the only logically consistent and morally sound way to define equity under current conditions is as maxim 3, payment according to effort. In the remainder of this chapter we therefore ask whether traditional economic institutions yield equitable outcomes in the sense of payment according to effort.

A variety of arguments indicate the desirability of attaining important goals that most traditional economists ignore. Besides equity, self-management (decision making input in proportion to degree affected), solidarity (granting others equal consideration in their endeavors), and variety (attaining a diversity of outcomes) are desirable. For example, more self-management is desirable, *ceteris paribus*, because we humans have the capacity to analyze and evaluate the consequences of our actions and choose accordingly, and we garner considerable satisfaction from doing so. Greater solidarity is desirable, *ceteris paribus*, because social esteem is an important source of human fulfillment and achieving it through invidious comparison is a zero or negative sum game, while achieving it through solidarity is a positive sum game. Finally, a variety of life-styles promotes sound ecology, assists in maximizing human well-being under conditions of uncertainty, and increases opportunities for another important source of human satisfaction, vicarious enjoyment. To add self-management, solidarity, and variety to the traditional list of valuative norms does not require that we argue that these goals can be maximized simultaneously any more than traditional theory must argue that equity and efficiency can be maximized simultaneously to include both as valuative norms. The point is only that self-management, solidarity, and variety are all legitimate valuative criteria for judging economic institutions. In short, human development characterized by self-management, solidarity, and variety is preferable, *ceteris paribus*, just as efficient allocations and equitable distributions are preferable, *ceteris paribus*. Asking whether particular institutions help people attain self-management, variety, and solidarity is sensible.

We also accept the traditional view that a desirable economy should be efficient. As long as resources are scarce relative to human needs and socially useful labor has burdensome components, efficiency is preferable to wastefulness, *ceteris paribus*. Moreover, we accept the concept Pareto optimality as a useful definition of social efficiency for most purposes. But since people are conscious agents whose characteristics and therefore preferences develop over time, to assess long-term efficiency we must assess the impact of economic institutions on people's development. In this regard, a series of theorems we have proved elsewhere usefully highlights the importance of institutional biases without assuming one kind of preference is "better" than another.[1]

Welfare Theorems with Endogenous Preferences

The view that people are self-conscious agents whose characteristics and preferences develop can be summarized in a model of "endogenous preferences." Using such a model we have demon-

---

1. See chapter 6 in Hahnel and Albert, *Quiet Revolution in Welfare Economics* (Princeton, N.J.: Princeton University Press, 1990), hereafter cited as *Welfare Economics*.

strated that in an economy that contains a bias in the relative terms of supply of two economic activities:

1. The degree of nonoptimality will be greater than indicated by traditional welfare theory and the divergence from optimality will "snowball" over time.

2. Individuals' human development patterns will be "warped" and the warping will "snowball" over time.

3. The effects of the bias in the economy will be disguised to participants who adjust unconsciously or forget they have adjusted after the fact.

The logic behind these new welfare theorems is that to the extent people recognize the "preference development" as well as "preference fulfillment" effects of their economic choices, it is sensible for them to take both effects into account when making decisions. If an economic institution is biased against some activity—that is, if it systematically charges people more than the true social opportunity cost of making the activity available to them—then rational people will choose activities in part to develop a lower preference for that activity than if they were charged the true social opportunity cost. It follows that the demand for the activity will be less than had people not adjusted their preferences. But this implies even less resources will be allocated to produce the activity than had people not adjusted. The ensuing misallocation of resources will further warp human characteristics, leading to further misallocation.

The theorems summarized above indicate that if an economic institution systematically biases the terms of availability of different economic options, the consequence will be a snowballing divergence from efficient allocations. This implies that a major factor in judging economic institutions should be determining whether they exert any systematic biases on individual choice.

In sum, to judge both traditional and new economic institutions, we will ask whether they subvert or promote:

1. Efficiency (where human characteristics and preferences can develop over time).

2. Equity (interpreted as payment according to effort).

3. Self-management (defined as decision making input in proportion to the degree one is affected).

4. Solidarity (defined as equal consideration for the well-being of others).

5. Variety (defined as a diversity of outcomes).

We will also ask if economic institutions impose any biases on individual choice that impede these five aims by charging people other than the true social opportunity costs for activities.

Allocation Institutions

Elsewhere we have examined markets and central planning in detail according to the above criteria.[1] A summary of our findings regarding markets is that the cybernetic, incentive, and allocative properties of markets involve a pervasive bias against discovering, expressing, and developing needs that require social rather than individual activity for their fulfillment. Markets do not provide concrete information about how my decisions affect the life prospects of others. They do not even provide accurate summaries of the social benefits and costs associated with what I decide to do since they misevaluate external effects, and external effects are the rule rather than the exception. Actual market allocations undersupply social goods and activities and oversupply individual goods and activities, thereby establishing incentives for individuals to wean themselves of needs that require socially coordinated intercourse for their fulfillment and accentuate needs that can be met individually. Moreover, markets reward competitive behavior and penalize cooperative behavior. In sum, markets not only erode solidarity, but systematically mischarge purchasers, so that over time preferences that are "individually rational" for people to develop combine with biases inherent in market allocations to yield outcomes increasingly further from those that would have maximized human fulfillment. In the end, the fears of "romantic" critics who decry the "socially

---

1. See chapters 7 and 9 in *Welfare Economics*.

alienating" effects of markets prove more to the point than the assurances of "scientific" economists that markets are ideal allocative institutions.

However, studies (and history) have revealed that the best-known alternative to markets is flawed as well. A summary of our case against central planning is that it necessarily generates authoritarian dynamics, minimizes the information that producers receive about their relations with others, and generates a monopoly of technical knowledge in the Central Planning Bureau. Central planning's inter-unit roles are command relationships that promote compatible hierarchies within production units. No matter how democratic procedures for determining the social welfare function planners attempt to maximize may be, central planning is ill suited to providing workers greater say over their own activities than over the activities of others. While traditional critics of central planning focus on information and incentive problems, we argue that central planning's "tragic flaw" is its bias against self-management and the authoritarian dynamics this entails.

While it would take us too far afield to reproduce our full critique of markets and central planning, since our conclusions diverge dramatically from traditional conclusions we outline our logic here.

Markets

The traditional view celebrates markets as socially neutral efficiency machines. In contrast, we discover a fatal antisocial bias that generates gross inefficiency.

Commodity Fetishism

Markets coordinate economic activity by providing separate units the opportunity to offer their outputs in exchange for the outputs of others. In any economy, the activity of any group would be impossible without inputs from other groups and outputs from one group would have no purpose were they not destined to be inputs for some other group. We easily understand that workers at the beginning and end of a GM assembly line undertake the connected social activity of making automobiles, but we have difficulty understanding that workers at U.S. Steel and at GM are similarly related. This "comprehension differential" arises because within local units we see that activities of different individuals are consciously coordinated to achieve a goal, while between units markets obscure our ability to see activities as joint endeavors. Outside each firm, relations between people and things or things and things remain evident, but relations between people and people are obscured. This, of course, has been termed "commodity fetishism," and its corrosive ills are independent of ownership relations. For workers to *comprehensively* evaluate their work they would have to know the human and social as well as material factors that went into the inputs they use as well as the human and social consequences their outputs make possible. But the only information markets provide, with or without private property, are the prices of the commodities people exchange. Even if these prices accurately reflect all the human and social relationships lurking behind economic transactions, they will not allow producers and consumers to adjust their activities in light of a *self-conscious* understanding of their relations with other producers or consumers. It follows that markets do not provide qualitative data necessary for producers to judge how their activities affect consumers or vice versa. The absence of information about the concrete effects of my activities on others leaves me little choice but to consult my own situation exclusively. But the individualism this leads to will impede solidarity and efficiency.

Antagonistic Roles

Lack of concrete qualitative information in market economies makes cooperation difficult, but competitive pressures make it individually irrational. Neither buyers nor sellers can afford to consider the situation of the other. Not only is relevant information unavailable, solidarity would be self-defeating. Polluters must try to hide their transgressions since paying a pollution tax or modernizing their equipment would lower profits. Even if one producer in an industry does not behave egocentrically, others will, and if the altruists persist in their socially responsible behavior they will ultimately be driven out of business for their trouble. In general, market competition militates against solidarity, again, regardless of ownership relations.

Markets and Workplace Hierarchy

The information, incentive, and role characteristics of markets also subvert the rationale for workers to take initiative in workplace decisions *even if* they have the legal right to do so. Workers' councils in Yugoslavia have the right to meet and make decisions, but why should they? Market competition forces decision makers to maximize a bottom line. Any human effects unrepresented in costs and revenues are ignored on pain of competitive failure. Workers' councils motivated by qualitative, human considerations ultimately fail, eliminating even their own information-limited generosity.

Since competitive pressures militate against criteria such as workplace satisfaction, it is perfectly sensible for workers' councils in market environments to hire others to make their decisions for them. The pattern is simple. First, worker desire for self-management erodes. Next, workers hire managers who in turn hire engineers and administrators who transform job roles according to competitive dictates. Even in the absence of private ownership, a process that begins with workers choosing to delegate technical and alienated decisions to experts ends by increasing the fragmentation of work, bloating managerial prerogatives, and substituting managers' goals for those of workers. It is not too long before a burgeoning managerial class of "coordinators" begins to maximize the size of the surplus earmarked for themselves and to search for ways to preserve their own social power.

Antisocial Bias

The last problem with markets is that they are biased against provision of goods with greater than average positive external effects. The fact that markets systematically overcharge users of goods with positive external effects and undercharge users of goods with negative external effects is well known to traditional economists. But what is not readily admitted is that external effects are the rule, not the exception, because this implies that market prices generally misestimate social benefits and costs and markets generally misallocate resources. Coupling recognition of this bias with an understanding that consumers eventually bend their preferences toward relatively less expensive offerings and away from relatively more expensive offerings helps explain why markets inexorably produce egocentric behavior and antisocial outcomes. Ironically, it turns out that once we account for the endogeneity of preferences and recognize the pervasiveness of externalities, markets not only impede solidarity, self-management, and equity, but generate misleading price signals and inefficient allocations as well.

Markets and Coordinatorism

In sum, theoretical analysis based on realistic assumptions about external effects and endogenous preferences suggests that even if capitalist owners are replaced by democratic workers' councils, market allocations disempower executionary workers and empower conceptual workers. That this can lead to popular apathy, egocentric personalities, and a new ruling class of coordinators is clear. And nothing in the historical experience of Yugoslavia suggests otherwise. Markets predictably generate pressures for class differentiation and intrinsically subvert equality, participation, and collective self-management.

Central Planning

It is well known that central planning cannot be efficient unless central planners:

1. Know the quantities of available resources and equipment.

2. Know the ratios in which production units can combine inputs to yield desired outputs.

3. Are informed of the relative social worths of final goods.

4. Have sufficient computing facilities to carry out elaborate quantitative manipulations.

5. Can impose incentives that will induce managers and workers to carry out their assigned tasks.

If we generously grant all these assumptions, central planners can calculate an efficient production plan and then choose from a variety of options for how to assign workers to jobs and distribute goods to consumers. But in all known versions of central planning:

1. The famous down/up down/up process is down-go-questions up-come-answers; down-go-orders up-comes-obedience.

2. Qualitative information essential to evaluating human outcomes is never generated, much less disseminated.

3. Elite "conceptual workers" monopolize what information is required for decision making.

4. The only management left to production units is to manage to fulfill centrally planned targets using allotted inputs.

Central planners issue "marching orders" and units obey. Each unit is subordinate to the planning board and since any superior agent must have effective means for holding subordinates accountable, methods of surveillance and verification are needed to minimize malfeasance. Central planners will prefer to appoint managers rather than establish complicated procedures to control rambunctious councils. And, having done so, central planners will logically wish to grant the managers they have appointed dictatorial powers over the workers in their employ.

Moreover, in real world central planning, planners can bias the "social welfare function" in favor of their interests. But even if we assume that planners forswear all opportunities to bias planning objectives, and even if goals are established by democratic voting procedures, two important defects remain.

1. Since most actors would still be denied access to quantitative information, and no one would have access to anything but the most cursory qualitative information, no citizen could intelligently determine her or his preferences in light of all social effects.

2. Since majority rule allocates the same influence over every decision to every voter, even "best case" central planning would fail to provide self-management since workers and consumers would not influence outcomes in proportion to the extent they are affected. That is, even though my opinion about my workplace should count more than someone else's opinion of *my* situation—just as their opinion should count more than mine about *their* workplace—everyone would have the same decision making input about production in every workplace if decisions are made by democratic voting

for the social welfare function which planners translate into a production plan.

Finally, as we discussed previously, in all economic systems individuals naturally orient their preferences toward opportunities that will be relatively plentiful and away from those that will be relatively scarce. If a bias arises in expected future supply of particular roles or goods, people will contour their development accordingly. In the case of central planning, the bias against providing self-managed work opportunities militates against people developing greater desires and capacities for self-management and promotes ever greater apathy instead. We have explained these tendencies at great length elsewhere.[1] But even the summary presented here should suffice to explain why central planning is likely to promote coordinator rule and skew economic outcomes.

In sum, markets systematically destroy solidarity while central planning systematically thwarts self-management. Both contain fundamental biases that generate increasingly nonoptimal outcomes and social dynamics that promote coordinator class rule. It follows that economies cannot employ either markets or central planning and expect to achieve participatory, egalitarian outcomes. Instead, if these goals are to be achieved, a new allocative procedure will have to be found.

Production and Consumption

Even if a participatory economy cannot use traditional allocative procedures, must we search for new ways of organizing production and consumption as well?

Private Ownership

For some, "freedom of enterprise" is a fundamental right as well as the cornerstone of political liberty. In this view, if people are not

---

1. In chapter 10 of *Welfare Economics* we examined the theoretical properties of central planning, and in Albert and Hahnel, *Socialism Today and Tomorrow* (Boston: South End Press, 1981) we analyzed the historical experiences of the Soviet Union, China, and Cuba.

free to hire any who are willing to work for them under conditions the employer specifies, people's fundamental economic freedoms are violated, and other freedoms are threatened as well. While we agree that economic freedom is a crucial valuative criterion and inextricably linked with political and cultural freedom, we do not accept the equation of economic freedom with freedom of enterprise, or the conclusion that private enterprise is compatible with economic freedom.

In our view, economic freedom is best defined as decision making input in proportion to the degree one is affected by the outcome of an economic choice, or as self-management. The problem with freedom of enterprise is that the "freedom" of employers inevitably conflicts with the "freedom" of employees. When stockholders exercise their freedom of enterprise to decide how *their* company will operate, they violate their employees' right to decide how *their* laboring capacities will be utilized. In other words, if production is organized under private ownership, the "property" rights of employers (freedom of enterprise) inevitably conflict with the "human" rights of employees (self-management). One way of explaining our position is that we accord human rights priority over property rights. A more philosophically consistent way of puting it is that we grant *all* the right of self-management, which is the only formulation of "economic freedom" that does not implicitly grant some people freedom at the expense of others.

The rebuttal of those who define economic freedom as freedom of enterprise is, of course, that employees are always free not to work for any particular employer, and free to become employers themselves if they wish. There are three problems with this response.

1. Unequal ownership of property is inconsistent with "equality of opportunity" to become an employer under the best of circumstances, and effectively limits the majority to choosing *which* employer will infringe upon their right of self-management in realistic settings.

2. Even if we started with equal ownership of property, maintaining equality of ownership entails redistributing people's property which supporters of freedom of enterprise oppose

as unjustifiable expropriation and a violation of people's right to dispose of their wherewithal without interference.

3. Even if equal opportunity to become an employer could be maintained, this merely grants all an equal chance to infringe on someone else's human right of self-management rather than have their own right of self-management violated. It is the logical equivalent of a fair lottery assigning people to be slave owners or slaves.

In any case, private ownership subverts self-management as we define it. It also subverts equity, defined as payment according to effort, since this maxim implies that income derived from ownership of property is unjustifiable, which we discuss at length in chapter 3.

Finally, there is a more subtle argument against private enterprise. Unless there is 100 percent labor turnover each time period, profit maximization under competitive conditions implies that any kind of laboring activity that generates employee empowering traits will have an actual market wage less than its socially optimal wage and be undersupplied by private employers, while any kind of labor activity that weakens employee empowering traits will be paid more than its socially optimal wage and be oversupplied by private employers.[1] Various writers from a school of economic analysis known as "the conflict theory of the firm" have argued plausibly, in our opinion, that work conditions under participatory, cooperative, and fair conditions constitute laboring activities of the first kind—which will be undersupplied according to our theorem—whereas work under discriminatory conditions or in situations with artificial hierarchies constitute laboring activities of the second kind, and will, therefore, be oversupplied. So the common thread running through the conflict school is that socially counterproductive and inefficient practices such as wage and employment discrimination, exaggerating hierarchies, and de-skilling the work force are part and parcel of profit maximization. Or, put differently, profit maximization under private enterprise undermines rather than promotes self-management and solidarity, and misallocates human productive potentials as well.

---

1. See theorem 8.1 in *Welfare Economics*.

However, even if private enterprise is ruled out on efficiency and equity grounds, as well as because it is inconsistent with self-management, it remains to assess traditional workplace structures that have existed in public as well as private enterprise environments and are generally considered an inevitable part of economic life.

Hierarchical Production

We leave to chapter 2 the question of whether production *can* be organized in ways that are nonhierarchical, and if so, whether this necessarily entails a loss of efficiency. Here we simply ask if hierarchical production relations are consistent with the goals of a participatory, equitable economy.

The answer is "no" for reasons that are obvious to most workers but apparently obscure to many economists. If someone's work is mechanical and mindless it will diminish her or his self-esteem, confidence, and self-management skills. On the other hand, if some-one's work is exciting and challenging, it will enhance her or his ability to analyze and evaluate economic alternatives. Hierarchical work leaves a differential imprint on personalities. For those at the top it yields an inquisitive, expansionist outlook. For those at the bottom it leaves an aggrieved and self-deprecating view. People's confidence or self-doubts, intelligence or ignorance, wisdom or foolishness all derive, in part, from the kind of economic activities they engage in. If an economy segregates the work force so that most people do rote work while only a few people engage in conceptual tasks, these opposed classes will inevitably develop unequal capacities to participate in economic decision making. Conversely, if we want to increase economic participation, we must arrange job complexes to be equally empowering.

Under hierarchical arrangements, many capable citizens enter industry only to exert little influence and do boring work. Those few who advance to more fulfilling and commanding jobs have freer workdays and greater "thinking" time than those who remain at the bottom. Each promotion increases immediate power and also the beneficiary's skill and information advantages for future competi-tions. Not only will this lead to disparate opportunities for participa-tion, but hierarchical production relations will generate inegalitarian outcomes as well. People who occupy favored positions in production hierarchies will appropriate more pleasant work conditions and greater consumption opportunities than those afforded their subordinates. And this will be the case whether the hierarchy is based on differential ownership or on differential access to information and decision making opportunities.

Consumption Institutions

Economists generally take consumption for granted and expend little energy evaluating consumption institutions. Since we recognize the social aspects of consumption activity obscured in the traditional economic paradigm and propose social institutions to coordinate "social" consumption, we must address the issue of the implications of hierarchical relations in consumption as well as production. Not surprisingly, we find that hierarchical consumption relations will create disproportionate input in decision making and inequality, so that if participatory equitable economies exist they must have nonhierarchical consumption relations.

Since the case that hierarchical relations of consumption subvert equal access to participation and equity is logically similar to the argument against hierarchical production relations, what remains to establish is the relevance of the problem in the case of consumption. Even in traditional economies that provide insufficient means for expressing and organizing social consumption, many consumption decisions are made by families and by various agencies of local, state, and federal government. In a traditional, patriarchal family there is a hierarchy of influence over consumption decisions in which the male head of household, wife, and children have degrees of authority that are not in proportion to the degree they are affected. Many traditional government procedures are far from democratic, and even when decisions are subject to one person one vote, to suggest that 79,000 Americans who earned the minimum wage in 1987 had the same influence over public consumption as Michael Milken, who "earned" as much as all of them combined, is highly disingenuous. So in traditional economies there is social consumption whose organization is hierarchical. And in participatory economies, where social consumption will receive greater attention, it will be even more important to ensure that consumption is not organized hierarchically. For hierarchy implies disparate influence that is uncorrelated with the degree people are affected, whether it be in context of production or consumption decision making.

The Logic of Power

While hierarchical production is logically conceivable alongside participatory and equitable consumption, and vice versa, there are good reasons to doubt that any real social formation could maintain such combinations. A hierarchy, anywhere, implies disparate influence over outcomes. Just as it is difficult to imagine that those with greater influence over production decisions would not eventually use their power to ensure themselves more pleasurable work situations, it is difficult to believe that those with greater power in one area of social life would not use their advantage to seek advantages elsewhere. Provided we remember that such efforts do not always succeed and that self-management can "spread" as well as disparate power can, we might refer to this logic as the "law" of institutional accommodation. Just as economic hierarchies in capitalist economies can subvert participatory politics, we should bear in mind that hierarchical relations in any part of the economy can subvert participatory, equitable, relations in the others. Not only must we rule out hierarchy in production, consumption, or allocation as subversive of participation and equity in other sectors of society, but as subversive of establishing and maintaining participation and equity in other aspects of the economy as well.

It follows that the arguments in this chapter, which we have presented elsewhere at great length, leave us no choice but to search for new institutions and procedures for organizing production, consumption, and allocation if we are to achieve efficiency, equity, self-management, solidarity, and variety. This we do throughout the rest of this book.

2

PRODUCTION

It is an abuse of words to apply the same term "discipline" to such unrelated concepts as the mindless reflex motions of a body with a thousand hands and a thousand legs, and the spontaneous coordination of the conscious political acts of a group of men.

—Rosa Luxemburg

Now, as to occupations, we shall clearly not be able to have the same division of labor as now: vicarious servanting, sewer-emptying, butchering, letter carrying, boot-blacking, hair-dressing, and the rest of it, will have come to an end...we shan't put a pattern on a cloth or a twiddle on a jug-handle to sell it, but to make it prettier and to amuse ourselves and others.

—William Morris

If hierarchical relations of production and segregation of conceptual and executionary labor are incompatible with economic justice, how can we organize work to be equitable, to allow workers who are prepared and inclined to participate in decision making to do so, *and* to ensure that *all* workers are prepared to partake in making decisions as well as in carrying them out?

Workers' Councils

The first step toward establishing nonhierarchical work is to establish workers' councils. Every workplace is governed by a workers' council in which each worker has one vote. Smaller councils are organized for divisions, units, and work teams as circumstances dictate. All issues are ultimately subject to majority rule in the workers' council, but this does not preclude establishing more refined procedures where different degrees of consensus make sense. In fact, forging a workplace decision making structure that allows people to influence decisions in proportion to the degree they are affected would almost always require more refined decision making than simple voting since not all workers are *equally* affected by all workplace decisions. By leaving decisions that only affect a subgroup of workers to those workers and their councils, by assigning initiative to those most affected by matters, and by weighing voting to reflect differential impacts, democratic workers' councils would fashion their own best approximation to self-management.

We claim neither that conceiving and agreeing on the most appropriate arrangement will be free of dispute within actual workers' councils, nor that any particular arrangement will be universally applicable. The first point is simply that meetings of workers' councils where each worker has one vote would be the final arbiter just as stockholders' meetings where each owner votes as many times as shares she or he owns are the final arbiter in privately owned enterprises. And the second point is that in a situation where each worker has an interest in self-management and none has disproportionate power, it is not unreasonable to hope that workers' councils will strive for decision making structures and ways to delegate authority that accord with self-management rather than establish hierarchies.[1]

But even procedures that poll council members in proportion as they are affected may not *ensure* collective self-management. If some people hold authoritative jobs while others only obey, even in formally democratic meetings people who hold more authoritative and information-rich jobs will exert more influence. Beneath formal democracy, a hierarchy of managers can still dominate deliberations.

---

1. For those familiar with John Rawls' idea of an "Original Position" and his argument that those in such a position would logically agree to the "liberty principle"—maximum liberty for each consistent with equal liberty for all—we might point out that the argument here is similar.

Democratic councils, therefore, do not by themselves ensure full participation. Additionally, the organization of work must guarantee that all members of councils are equipped to express their desires and opinions.

Work Organization

We know that not all work is equally desirable and that even in formally democratic councils rote workers will lack the information, skills, and energies to participate equally with conceptual workers. Democratic councils help foster participation and equity but something must equalize daily work assignments so the impact of people's work experience does not destroy equity and self-management. If some have greater information and responsibility to use to their advantage to dominate policy making, they can become a ruling "coordinator class," both thwarting workers' participation and monopolizing desirable work roles.

Balanced Job Complexes

The remedy is conceptually simple: If you work at a particularly unpleasant or disempowering task, you should spend some time working at other more pleasant or empowering tasks as well. Pleasant and unpleasant work, rote work and conceptual or administrative work must be balanced. People should not do one type all the time. To foster participation and equity people must be assigned to a balanced mix of tasks. Which is not to say every person must perform every task in every workplace. This is impossible and unnecessary. The same person need not work as a doctor, an engineer, and a literary critic, and those who assemble cars today need not assemble computers tomorrow. Nor should everyone who works in a hospital perform brain surgery. The point is simply that people should rotate in some reasonable time period through some sequence of tasks for which they are adequately trained so that no one enjoys consistent advantages over others.

However, we are not merely suggesting that doctors occasionally clean bed pans or that secretaries attend an occasional seminar. Parading through the ghetto does not yield scars and slinking through the country club does not confer status. Short-term stints in alternative circumstances do not rectify inequalities in basic responsibilities. Likewise, for those doing elite work in one workplace to do rote work in another does not challenge mystification, deference, and authoritarianism in *either* workplace. Only primary job complexes balanced for desirability and empowerment can give all workers an equal chance of participating in and benefiting from workplace decisions.

Since disparate empowerment destroys participatory potentials and creates class differences that in turn lead to inequity, we focus on empowerment without implying that balancing to rectify differential desirabilities is not also important. But balancing for empowerment is more complicated and solutions are also applicable to balancing for equity. Likewise, for the reasons noted above, our initial focus is each individual's *primary* responsibility. Is it a number of different rote tasks, a number of different skilled tasks, or a combination of diverse tasks in a single package balanced with others in the unit for empowerment?

Whereas capitalist and coordinator jobs combine tasks with the same qualitative characteristics so that each worker has a homogeneous job complex and most people do *one* level of task, in contrast, participatory jobs combine tasks into balanced job complexes where everyone does *many* levels of tasks. Everyone works at a particular bundle of diverse tasks, but all bundles prepare people to participate as equals in democratic workplace decision making.

While one might question the efficiency of organizing workplaces and industries this way, it is certainly theoretically possible. Formally, for any economy E:

1. We construct the set of all possible single types of productive activities, {PA}.

2. We construct the subsets of "practically identical production activities" of {PA}, ${PIPA}^i$, where each member of each ${PIPA}^i$ has essentially the same qualitative effect on workers as any other member of that subset, and a different effect than any member of any other practically identical subset, ${PIPA}^j$, so that:

    i. The set of all practically identical activities subsets of {PA} constitutes a partition of {PA}.

    ii. The subsets $\{PIPA\}^i$ can be ordered along a spectrum of qualitative effects on workers ranging from empowering to debilitating.

The critical practical issue in creating this spectrum of subsets of activities is how finely to measure "qualitative effects." If we measure too precisely, each $\{PIPA\}^i$ will have only one element. If we measure too flexibly, each $\{PIPA\}^i$ will be huge. Both partitions would be useless. In practice, experience and special evaluative boards would settle this matter. In theory, there is no problem.

3. We construct the menu of available job complexes by combining different productive activities from different subsets of practically identical production activities to form balanced job complexes so that the menu of available job complexes includes only offerings that incorporate a mix of tasks which together have comparably empowering effects.

It is useful to note that we can learn much about the social relations, human effects, and class structure of any economy by examining its menu of available job complexes. Suppose, as in capitalism *and* coordinatorism, a few elements of the menu of available job complexes combine tasks that all come from $\{PIPA\}^i$s high on the empowerment spectrum, and most combine tasks that all come from $\{PIPA\}^j$s low on the empowerment spectrum. However talents among participants in the economy may be initially dispersed, eventually a work force assigned roles from this menu will divide into classes enjoying disparate decision making input and receiving unequal rewards. Alternatively, if all elements from an economy's job complex menu are equally empowering, even a work force that begins with disparate decision making abilities will move toward nonhierarchical participation, the hallmark of a truly participatory economy.

Balancing Across Workplaces

In balancing job complexes within each workplace for equal empowerment, the goal was to prevent the organization and assignment of tasks *within* a workplace from preparing some workers better than others to participate in decision making. But balancing job complexes for empowerment within workplaces does not guarantee that work life will be equally empowering across workplaces, any more than balancing job complexes for desirability within work-places guarantees that working in different industries will be equally desirable. Establishing conditions for a participatory, equitable economy requires *overall* balance in addition to balance *within* each workplace. Clearly, to guarantee equal opportunity to participate both within units *and* in the economy as a whole requires internal as well as overall balance. Strictly speaking, overall balance for desirability is sufficient for work equity. But since, in practice, this will usually be easiest to achieve by arranging internal balance regarding desirability and then correcting for differences between workplaces, the conclusion that a participatory, equitable economy requires approximate internal *and* external balance for both em-powerment and desirability is a useful rule of thumb.

The only way to balance for desirability and empowerment *across* workplaces is to have people spend time outside their primary workplace. How can an economy accomplish this? How can it calibrate balance? For that matter, how do people come to work in one or another workplace in the first place?

In a participatory economy, everyone will have the right to apply to work wherever they choose, and every workers' council will have the right to add any members they choose. We must wait until after explaining participatory allocation to analyze when and why workers' councils would wish to add or release members, but for now it is sufficient to know that once the plan is finalized, each workers' council will have a list of openings for which all can freely apply. So any worker can apply for any opening, and move to a new workers' council that wants them should they prefer it to their present council.

While this resembles traditional labor markets, much is different. Under traditional labor markets people generally change employ-ment to win higher pay or enjoy more desirable working conditions. But if a participatory, equitable economy balances job complexes across as well as within workplaces, and if equitable consumption requires "equal pay for equal effort," people will be unable to attain these traditional goals by changing workplaces. This is not to say people will never change workplaces in a participatory, equitable economy. If a person would prefer a different group of workmates, or working at a different combination of tasks, she or he would have good reason to apply for membership in a different workers' council. But to the extent job complexes are balanced, these personal preferences will be the only motives to move, and, conversely, the freedom to move will provide a check on the effectivness of efforts to balance for equity across workplaces. Higher pay will not be available by changing jobs, nor will objectively better work conditions, since pay and conditions will be balanced.

Just as workers must balance complexes internally through a rating process, so will delegates of workers from different councils and industries develop a rating process to balance across workplaces. There will thus be "Job Complex Committees" both within each workplace and for the economy as a whole. The internal committees will combine tasks and assign work times to achieve balanced work complexes within workplaces. The economywide committee will assign workers in less desirable and less empowering primary workplaces offsetting time in more desirable and empowering environments, and, vice versa, it will also assign workers in more desirable and empowering primary workplaces offsetting time in less desirable and empowering environments. The check on internal calibration will be whether more members of a workers' council want one assignment or another. The check on overall balance will be excessive applications to change workplaces. Economywide committees will adjust rotation times to eliminate significant discrepancies in people's applications to work in different workplaces.

Balance in Practice

Creating balanced job complexes is theoretically possible. And if we combine balanced job complexes with democratic councils, we would have nonhierarchical production relations that promote equity and participation. But in practical situations, could workers really rate and combine tasks to define balanced complexes within and across plants?

Provided we are talking about a social process that never attains perfection, but does fulfill workers' own sense of balance, the answer is yes. The idea is that workers within a plant would engage in a collective evaluation of their own circumstances. As a participatory economy emerged from a capitalist or coordinator past, naturally there would be a lengthy discussion and debate about the characteristics of different tasks. But once the first approximation of balanced complexes within a workplace had been established, yearly adjustments would be relatively simple. If the introduction of a new technology changed the human impact of some task, thereby throwing old complexes out of balance, workers would simply move some tasks among affected complexes or change the time spent at different tasks in affected complexes to attain a new balance.

The new balance need not be perfect, nor the adjustments instantaneous, nor would everyone need to agree completely with the result of a democratic determination. As a matter of fact, individual preferences that deviate from one's workmates would determine *who* would choose to apply for *which* balanced complexes. If I am less bothered by noise but more bothered by dust than most, I will apply for a complex whose rote component is attending noisy machinery rather than a complex with a sweeping detail.

In practice balancing *between* workplaces would be more complicated. How would arrangements be made for workers to have responsibilities in more than one workplace? Over time, balancing across workplaces would be determined partly as a result of a growing familiarity with the social relations of production, partly as a result of evaluations by committees whose job is to rate complexes in different plants and industries, and partly as a result of the pattern of movement of workers. Since workers are free to apply for complexes within their workplace, and free to "vote with their feet" by seeking work in other workplaces, there is "oversight" for the collective decision making process.

That all this is possible, within some acceptable range of error and degree of dissent ought to be obvious.[1] Job complexes *could* be organized so every individual would be regularly involved in both

---

1. Those interested in the details of how all this might be accomplished and what the result might look like in different workplaces and industries should see Albert and Hahnel, *Looking Forward: Participatory Economics for the Twenty First Century* (Boston: South End Press, 1991).

conception and execution. No individual *need* permanently occupy positions that present unusual opportunities to accumulate influence or knowledge. The human costs and benefits of work *could* be equitably distributed. But do balanced work complexes have inherent disadvantages that outweigh their advantages?

Participation Versus Efficiency

We have argued that balancing work complexes for empowerment is a necessary condition for guaranteeing all actors equal opportunity to participate in economic decision making. But many believe that this would destroy efficiency. In our own view, the relation between participation and efficiency will more likely be positive than negative, but in any case it is more complicated than contemporary "common wisdom" asserts.

One prevalent view has it that some people make decisions better than others, so that the only efficient arrangement is for them to make all important decisions. In other words, participatory decision making is inherently inefficient since it gives everyone decision making input proportional to the degree she or he is affected even though some people make decisions better than others. Of course, this was the same argument used to support the rule of kings against demands for popular representation, the rule of "wise" and "benevolent" dictators against demands for democracy, the rule of men against demands for women's suffrage, and the rule of a "vanguard" party against demands for political pluralism. Do those who accept the wisdom of universal suffrage, democracy, and political pluralism do so at the expense of efficiency? Does some distinction between political and economic decisions warrant popular participation in the former but not the latter?

Human beings have the potential to make conscious choices in light of our understanding of the consequences of alternatives. Particular social environments can subvert or suppress this potential in the majority as when political dictatorship, patriarchy, dogmatic religions, slavery, and authoritarian education stifle people's decision making potentials. But one important goal of desirable social institutions is that they develop rather than thwart our most creative potentials. If we assume that noneconomic institutions develop these potentials, and if we choose economic institutions that do likewise, it is reasonable to assume participants would be capable of making economic choices in light of predicted consequences.

This is not to assert that everyone is equally knowledgable about every decision, or to deny a role for "expertise" in economic decision making. We often need "experts" to interpret the consequences of choices and to explain the likely implications of possible decisions. If experience shows a greater role for expertise in economic decisions than in political or other decisions, so be it. But once consequences are known because ordinary people have had the opportunity to hear diverse expert opinions, what remains is for the affected people to register their choices. While those with expertise in a particular matter may well predict consequences more accurately, those affected know best whether *they* prefer one outcome or another. In other words, making economic choices entails both *determining* consequences and *evaluating* them. While efficiency requires an important role for experts in determining complicated consequences, efficiency also requires that those who will be affected decide which consequences they prefer. Therefore, it is just as inefficient to keep those affected by decisions from making them after experts have analyzed and debated consequences, as it is to prevent experts from explaining and debating consequences of complicated choices before those affected register their desires. In sum, for *informed* self-management, there is no conflict between participation and efficiency.

Still, there is a sense in which guaranteeing the conditions necessary for establishing a fully participatory economy might be at the expense of efficiency. If a specific skill is scarce—either because an essential innate talent is only present in a fraction of the work force, or because training required to develop the skill is time consuming for trainees or trainer and less pleasurable than alternative human activities—then balancing work complexes for empowerment by assigning someone with this talent or training to work at an activity that requires a less scarce skill would be inefficient. Even so, assignments of this type might be *less* inefficient than any humanly feasible alternative. For example,

1. If always working at the same task proved so monotonous and boring that people's concentration, effort, and performance deteriorated, balancing might be more efficient than not balancing.

2. If failure to balance was deemed unfair, and resentment led to deteriorating performance on others' part, it is possible for balancing to be more efficient than nonbalancing.

3. If working at a complex including a number of tasks provides an overview of how different tasks depend on one another thereby enhancing the intelligence of people's efforts in their primary responsibilities, then even for the most skilled balancing might be more efficient than not.

4. If performance is positively correlated with participation, and participation is positively correlated with balancing, balanced complexes might prove more efficient than un-balanced complexes.

Besides a remarkable propensity not to consider these possibil-ities, the traditional view of the relation between job-mixing and efficiency rests on questionable assumptions regarding talent and training. In the traditional view, many productive talents are assumed present in only tiny fractions of the population, while most training is assumed terribly burdensome. Since doctors changing bed pans is an example those opposed to job balancing like to cite, it is not inappropriate to point out:

1. Ample experience demonstrates that it is possible to train only moderately good students to become physicians, so the "talent" necessary to become a doctor is apparently distri-buted among a rather large fraction of the population, and the inefficiency of having doctors change bed pans could be greatly reduced by training more doctors.

2. Protests of medical students aside, a substantial portion of medical training could be highly illuminating and have a positive "consumption" component so that the time occupied in the training process need not be as burdensome as the AMA would have us believe.

3. There is an implicit assumption that while it is inefficient for doctors to change bed pans, it is not inefficient for others to change them. However, while it is true that in societies where a large number of perfectly talented members of the work force receive no training, the opportunity costs of having them change bed pans are obviously less than the opportunity costs of doctors doing so, this would not hold if everyone received ample training in some area for which they had relevant talent. If all have their particular talents trained, there would be significant opportunity costs no matter who changed bed pans. As to whether it is more efficient for an economy to train all in accord with their talents, or more efficient to train the productive talents of only a few, the answer is obvious.

In sum, the "scarce talent" argument against balancing job complexes hinges on the assumption that a great deal of the work force has no trainable talents, while the "training cost" argument against balancing for empowerment ignores the fact that training can be quite enjoyable. Moreover, the claim that balancing is necessarily inefficient also ignores a number of ways in which balancing may improve performance that should be weighed against any opportunity costs that may exist.

In any case, we do not claim there are never opportunity costs to having people work outside their area of comparative advantage. We only claim that the case against balancing on efficiency grounds has been greatly exaggerated. In a society that provides all with appropriate training delivered in the most enjoyable rather than most distasteful ways, the opportunity costs of arranging job complexes with balanced empowerment are not likely to be anything like what opponents claim. Any losses in efficiency should be weighed against the importance of participation and reductions in coercive management needed to extract effort from recalcitrant "underlings."

Equity Versus Efficiency

We believe: (1) an equitable economy requires that people's work experiences be equally desirable, and (2) an equitable economy can be fully efficient. However, some economists dispute the conclusion that equitable means equal, and even among those who agree that equitable means equal, many believe an equitable economy must be inefficient due to lack of "material" incentives. Since the debate over what constitutes an equitable system of rewards, and the debate over the relation between "material" incentives and efficiency are the same whether we are talking about more desirable work conditions or greater consumption opportunities, we defer this issue to chapter 3 where we explore the meaning and consequences of insisting on equitable consumption opportunities. The conclusions we reach regarding equity and efficiency in consumption apply as well to equity and efficiency in work.

Information and Incentives

We would like workers to govern their activities in light of the full social costs of preparing the inputs they use, the social benefits of the outputs they make, and the costs in their time, energy, and the like, of doing the work. This entails evaluating a great deal of both qualitative and quantitative information. And while workers can best estimate the human effects of different options on themselves, the qualitative and quantitative consequences for others are not something we can expect workers to either know or respect unless the allocation system provides the necessary information and incentives. We argued in chapter 1 that neither central planning nor markets provide the necessary information and incentives for workers to make socially responsible decisions. Whether or not our allocation system will provide means and incentives for workers' councils to make decisions according to the criterion of *overall* social costs and benefits remains to be seen.

Choice of Technology

A new technology is superior if it yields greater net social benefits than existing ones. The simplest kinds of superior technologies use less of some scarce input without using more of any other input, or yield more of some desirable output without yielding less of any other output. These "pure input saving" and "pure output enhancing" techniques are probably not the most common superior technologies, although interestingly enough, new organizations of production that increase opportunities for workers' participation can often be counted among them. However, most new technologies use less of some inputs, but more of others, or generate more of some outputs but less of others. In these cases, whether the new technology is superior depends on whether the social cost of the inputs saved outweighs the social cost of the inputs used, or whether the social benefit of the outputs increased outweighs the social benefit of the outputs lost.

Whether the information available and incentives for those who choose technologies in different kinds of economies can be relied on to lead them always and only to implement superior techniques is, of course, of great concern. John Roemer presents an interesting model in which capitalist economies fail to achieve these goals whenever the rate of profit exceeds the growth rate.[1] Moreover, numerous proponents of the "conflict theory of the firm" have suggested that capitalists will not always choose superior techniques for reasons additional to the one Roemer analyzed.[2] And we have clarified the logic of why capitalists, even under competitive conditions, will reject superior techniques if they are sufficiently worker empowering.[3] On the other hand, our analysis of coordinator economies concludes that choice of technique in those systems will also be biased against worker empowering technologies.[4] While the full explanation of why we believe our participatory economy will implement superior techniques must wait until we present our allocation procedure, it should be clear that there is no reason for

---

1. See theorem 4.9, John Roemer, *Analytical Foundations of Marxian Economic Theory* (Cambridge: Cambridge University Press, 1981), 102-3. While Roemer's model assumes one primary input, homogeneous labor, we see no reason the problem he illustrates should not obtain in more realistic settings.
2. For example, see Herb Gintis, "The Nature of the Labor Exchange and the Theory of Capitalist Production," *Review of Radical Political Economics 8*, no. 2 (Summer 1976).
3. Theorem 8.1, *Welfare Economics*.
4. Theorem 9.1, *Welfare Economics*.

workers' councils to be biased against superior technologies because they are worker empowering! Moreover, since the criteria of choice are different, there is every reason to expect technologies developed in participatory economies to diverge from those that have developed in capitalist and coordinator systems. Over time this could dramatically improve the nature and quality of work life.

Diversity

It is important to note that nothing we have said implies that workers in different workplaces must make decisions or organize job complexes entirely alike. There will be a variety of ways workers can pursue the principles discussed in this chapter, so that each participatory workplace will optimize within constraints imposed by the allocation system, but according to the tastes of their own council members. Differences in workers' preferences and leeway in the constraints on council decision making will permit technologies *and* social relations to vary from workplace to workplace.

3

CONSUMPTION

Saemtenevia Prospect was two miles long, and it was a solid mass of things to buy, things for sale. Coats, dresses, gowns, robes, trousers, breeches, clothes to wear while sleeping, while swimming, while playing games, while at an afternoon party, while at an evening party, while at a party in the country, while traveling, while at the theater, while riding horses, gardening, receiving guests, dining, hunting—all different, all in hundreds of different cuts, styles, colors, textures, materials. But to Shevek the strangest thing about the nightmare street was that none of the millions of things for sale were made there. They were only sold there. Where were the workmen, the miners, the weavers, the chemists, the carvers, the dyers, the designers, the machinists, where were the hands, the people who made? All the people in all the shops were either buyers or sellers. They had no relation to the things but that of possessions. How was he to know what a good's production entailed? How could they expect him to decide if he wanted something?

—Ursula LeGuin

The traditional treatment of consumption is quite simple. As long as people are free to buy what they want in competitive markets, consumption will efficiently take care of itself. In this view, the only problem is that people's ability to buy—the distribution of income—may be inequitable. In this chapter we present the case for equity as payment according to effort, criticize the reasoning behind alternative definitions of equity, and examine whether an equitable economy lacks sufficient incentives to be a productive economy. However, while we focus on the meaning of equity and its implications, we do not think consumption takes care of itself efficiently when people simply buy what they want in markets. On the contrary, using markets to organize consumption is highly inefficient and exerts a deleterious bias on the development of people's preferences for reasons explained in chapter 1. So before tackling questions of equity, since externalities in consumption are the rule rather than the exception, and since the market's bias against goods and services with positive external effects provides socially counterproductive incentives for people to develop along trajectories that lead to ever greater losses in potential well-being, how can we organize consumption activity to minimize these failings? The answer lies in recognizing that much consumption activity, like much production activity, is social and should be organized as such.

Consumption Councils

Instead of markets, our principal means of organizing consumption activity are consumption councils. Every individual, family, or living unit would belong to its neighborhood consumption council. Each neighborhood council would belong to a federation of neighborhood councils the size of a city ward or a rural county. Each ward would belong to a city consumption council, each city and county council would belong to a state council, and each state council would belong to the national council.

Participatory economies incorporate this nesting of different consumers' councils to allow for the fact that different kinds of consumption affect different numbers of people. The color of my underwear concerns only me and my most intimate acquaintances. The shrubbery on my block concerns all who live on the block. The quality of play equipment in a park affects all in the neighborhood. The number of volumes in the library and teachers in the high school affect all in a ward. The frequency and punctuality of buses and subways affect all in a city. The disposition of waste affects all States in a major watershed. "Real" national security affects all citizens in a country, and protection of the ozone layer affects all humanity—

—40—

which means that my choice of deodorant, unlike my choice of underwear, concerns more than me and my intimates!

Failure to arrange for all those affected by consumption activities to participate in choosing them not only implies an absence of self-management, but, if the preferences of some are disregarded, also a loss of efficiency. It is to accommodate the range of consumption activities from the most private to the most public that we organize different "levels" of consumption councils. Once we recognize that much consumption activity, like production activity, is social, we must insist that consumption decision making, like production decision making, be participatory and equitable. And we must again investigate whether this is compatible with efficiency.

The principle of one person one vote will apply in all consumers' councils and federations of councils, and each consumers' council and consumers' federation will participate in the planning procedure described in chapter 4. In each iteration of the planning procedure, neighborhood councils will propose individual consumption requests for members as well as neighborhood consumption requests; ward councils will ask for inputs required to carry out consumption activities affecting all in a ward; city consumption councils will ask for inputs needed for consumption activities affecting all who live in a city, and so on. Every council must eventually win approval for its proposal from other councils. This means a neighborhood consumption council must win approval from the other neighborhood councils in its ward, ward councils must win approval from the other ward councils in the city, and so on. Moreover, consumers' councils must win approval of their proposals from workers' councils and vice versa. So consumption councils must demonstrate that their requests do not entail greater social costs per member than the requests of other consumption councils. Or, if a request does have a higher social cost than average, the council will have to provide an explanation others find acceptable. How consumers calculate and compare social costs of consumption requests will be explained when we describe allocation in chapter 4.

In neighborhood councils, each living unit will propose its own consumption request and while the content of individual proposals is open to discussion, requests whose social cost is no greater than the average individual consumption request cannot, in the end, be rejected by a neighborhood council.[1] In higher level consumption councils, each lower level council will "vote" its preferences either directly or by sending representatives, and lower level councils will be "charged" in the planning procedure for their proportionate share of the social cost of all public goods requested by higher level federations to which they belong, as described in chapter 4.

In light of the importance of representing consumers' interests in the economy, lower level consumption councils will have research and development task forces and higher level consumption councils will have full time R&D units. These R&D task forces and units will explore new consumption possibilities and ways to organize consumption so as to minimize wasteful duplication of goods, and will help establish priorities for R&D units attached to workers' councils and industry federations.

But "equal consumption rights" does not guarantee equal participation in consumption decision making. We doubt the problem is serious enough to require carefully calculated "consumption complexes" analogous to job complexes where consumption activity would be self-consciously balanced for empowerment, but certainly care should be taken to ensure that the same people do not always chair discussions, serve on research and development task forces, or serve as delegates to higher level consumer federations. Otherwise, they could accumulate disproportionate influence over consumption decisions.

Admittedly, there is a fine line between doing what is necessary to ensure that all are able to participate fully and infringing on individuals' rights to decide how often they want to attend meetings, serve on committees, and the like. In the final analysis, we would not propose granting consumers' councils the power to force a member to participate beyond her or his wishes. But it is interesting to note that to the extent that a participatory economy is a "public good" rather than merely a right guaranteed to those who choose to exercise it, an economic rationale exists for institutional forms that establish at least the expectation of participation on everyone's part.

---

1. We assume for the remainder of this chapter that consumers exert average effort in work. Appropriate adjustments would be made in any other event.

Incentive Compatibility

Efficient provision of public goods has never been considered easy. Before the literature on incentive compatible mechanisms there was a consensus among public finance theorists that while efficient allocations existed and could be identified in theory, the "free rider" problem would inevitably prevent achieving efficient allocations in practice. In *Welfare Economics* we have analyzed, interpreted, and evaluated the literature on incentive compatible mechanisms for providing public goods that blossomed at the end of the 1970s only to fall into oblivion in the 1980s because of their presumed impracticality. What we wish to point out here is that while our network of consumers' councils does not solve the problem perfectly (since an infinite spectrum of consumers' councils is a practical impossibility), our system for structuring consumption choices *is* compatible with "truthful" reporting of preferences for public goods. Moreover, our consumers' councils provide a practical setting for implementing some of the refinements brought to light by demand-revealing and pivot mechanisms.

While a full explanation must await our description of participatory allocation, there is no incentive for consumers in our economy to misrepresent their preferences regarding public goods at any level. Since each will be "charged" their proportionate share for the public goods proposed by the higher level councils to which they belong, there is no incentive to misrepresent preferences for public goods because there is no possibility of "riding free." The best way to influence the package of public goods one will consume is to vote truthfully. But while our system is incentive compatible with reasonable claims to efficiency, it "charges" people independent of their preferences. As we discussed elsewhere, the important issue raised by demand-revealing and pivot mechanisms is not efficiency, since there are simpler ways to achieve efficiency, but whether those whose preferences for public goods deviate further from average preferences should be "compensated" for their lesser benefits or be "charged" for skewing the package provided further away from the package others would have preferred.[1] "Outliers" will find the

---

1. See chapter 7 of *Welfare Economics.*

package of public goods less to their liking than those with average preferences, but "outliers" also inconvenience others more than those with average preferences when each expresses their preferences for public goods.

We also explained in *Welfare Economics* why an endogenous view of preferences changes one's view of what is at stake in implementing a "compensating" or "penalizing" system of assessing deviant preferences for public goods. A plausible case can be made for both compensating and penalizing on equity grounds. But if deviant preferences are penalized, people will develop more conformist tastes for public goods, whereas if deviant preferences are compensated, preference variety will be encouraged. While in our view more variety is generally better, in the case of public goods the more alike people's preferences are the easier it is to give everyone what they want. So it is not obvious what kind of deviations might be warranted from proportionate charges. But while there is no clear-cut theoretical answer to what adjustments should be made, this does not mean proportionate assessment cannot be improved on in particular situations. What should be more feasible in our system of consumers' councils, where people meet and discuss options and where people's preferences for public goods are explicitly recorded, is for consumers to debate the pros and cons of differential charges and make whatever compensations they deem warranted in the particular councils and federations to which they belong. What the theoretical literature on demand-revealing and pivot mechanisms has shown is that this can be done in incentive compatible ways. While implementing these procedures is impractical in traditional economies, our consumers' councils provide a practical setting for implementing these schemes whenever they are deemed beneficial by a particular group of consumers even though no single scheme can claim superiority in all situations.

Equity

Economists are not alone in being unable to agree on what constitutes equitable rewards. In fact, it was largely because philosophers, politicians, and people from all walks of life were as likely to disagree about what was equitable as economists were, that separating equity from efficiency via the concept of Pareto optimality was considered such a great theoretical advance. Nor do we expect everyone to agree with our conclusions regarding equity. Instead, we mainly wish to clarify an array of different options and the rationales behind each.

Distributive justice is only an issue in social arrangements where the human costs and benefits of joint endeavors must be assigned. In *Welfare Economics* we identified four different distributive maxims and noted that each justifies the outcomes of a different kind of economy.

DISTRIBUTIVE MAXIM 1. Payment according to personal contribution *and* the contribution of property owned.

DISTRIBUTIVE MAXIM 2. Payment according to personal contribution.

DISTRIBUTIVE MAXIM 3. Payment according to effort.

DISTRIBUTIVE MAXIM 4. Payment according to need.

Private enterprise, market economies distribute consumption opportunities according to Maxim 1. Public enterprise, market economies distribute according to Maxim 2. What we deem equitable economies distribute according to Maxim 3. Truly humane economies distribute according to Maxim 4.

We certainly do not intend to argue against Maxim 4. In situations where trust, empathy, and mutual concern—or what we call solidarity—are sufficient to permit distribution according to need, it will be pointless to do otherwise. Nor do we think such situations can only exist among family members, or small groups of intimate acquaintenances. Beyond participation and equity, an important goal for a desirable economy is to establish conditions giving rise to increasing solidarity among its participants since more fulfilling lives for all are possible when this holds. But for now we set Maxim 4 aside on grounds that it is beyond equity. It is not a conception of equity as much as a (fortunate) situation in which equity is no longer an issue.

For as long as justice or equity is an issue, what rationales support Maxims 1, 2, and 3? The rationale supporting Maxim 1 is that people should get out of an economy what they and their belongings contribute to it. It generally envisages "free and independent" people, each with his or her own property, who would refuse to enter a social contract on any other terms.

While it is clear that those who wander in the "state of nature" with a great deal of productive property would have reason to hold out for a social contract along the lines of Maxim 1, why those who wander in the "state of nature" with little on their backs would not hold out for a different arrangement is unclear. In other words, if the idea is that the social contract must be unanimous, it is not obvious why poorer inhabitants would agree to Maxim 1. Of course, if it is further stipulated that those with considerable wherewithal can do quite well for themselves in the "state of nature," whereas those without cannot, it is not difficult to see how requiring unanimity might drive the bargain in the direction of Maxim 1. However, for those of us who see nothing fair or equitable about a bargaining situation requiring unanimity when some are better able to tolerate failure to reach an agreement than others, the traditional version of a social contract rationale for Maxim 1 loses force. In any event, economists know that the marginal productivity of an input depends as much on the number of units of that input and other inputs available as on any intrinsic qualities of the input itself, which undermines the moral imperative many noneconomists assume behind Maxim 1. And Joan Robinson pointed out long ago that however "productive" a piece of land or machine may be, that hardly constitutes a reason for paying anything to its owner. As John Roemer has recently clarified, the morality of unequal income distributions due to unequal ownership of productive property therefore reduces to the morality of why the ownership is unequal in the first place.[1] It seems clear to us that unless those with more productive property acquired it through some greater sacrifice, the income they accrue from property is not justifiable, at least on equity grounds. In which case we must reject Maxim 1 if we find that those

---

1. See John Roemer, *Free to Lose* (Cambridge: Harvard University Press, 1988), chapter 5.

who own more productive property do not come by it through personal sacrifice, except in rare instances.

Inheritance of property hardly qualifies as a sacrifice by the heir. Moreover, in our view any "right to bequeath" of older generations should be subordinate to the "right of equal opportunity" of younger generations. We also believe most initial accumulations are more often the result of "robbery and plunder," unfair advantage, or simply good luck—none of which merit reward—rather than personal sacrifice. Moreover, as we will argue below, "unfair advantage" includes any accumulations due to personal attributes that were not acquired through personal sacrifice. To put it differently, in our view, whatever differences in productive property accumulate within a single generation due to uneven sacrifices are insignificant compared to the total differences in wealth that inevitably develop in private enterprise economies. In sum, we reject Maxim 1 on the grounds that "property is theft," more often than not, which means the resulting income is exploitation.

While those who support Maxim 2 find "property income" unjustifiable, they hold that all have a right to the "fruits of their labor." There is no doubt the rationale for this has a powerful appeal: If my labor contributes more to the social endeavor it is only right that I receive more. Not only am I not exploiting others, they would be exploiting me by paying me less than my contribution.[1] But, ironically, the same logic for rejecting Maxim 1 applies to Maxim 2. While we agree that greater personal sacrifice for the sake of the joint endeavor merits greater compensation, it turns out that most reasons why some contribute more than others have little to do with greater sacrifice on their part.

Besides the well-known fact that the marginal productivity of different kinds of labor depends greatly on the number of people in each category and the quantity of nonlabor inputs available to use, most differences in productivity due to "intrinsic" qualities cannot be traced to differential sacrifices. No amount of eating and weight lifting will give an average sized individual a 6 foot 7 inch frame

---

1. Interestingly enough, Mikhail Gorbachev provides one of the most eloquent, recent versions of this argument in *Perestroika: New Thinking for Our Country and the World* (New York: Harper and Row, 1987).

with 300 pounds of muscle. Yet, Dave Butz received over 50 times an average U.S. income for playing defensive tackle for the Washington Redskins largely because those attributes made his marginal revenue product outrageously high in the context of U.S. sports culture. Likewise, if the movie *Amadeus* is true to history, no matter how hard he tried, Salieri could never have turned out the music that leaped from the pen of his rival, Mozart, which continues to yield incalculable pleasure. Clearly, the genetic lottery greatly influences how valuable one's contributions will be. Yet there is nothing more fair about the genetic lottery than the inheritance lottery.

Frequently it is argued that while talent may not deserve reward, talent requires training, and herein lies the sacrifice that merits compensation. Doctors' salaries are compensation for all those years of education. And if it was truly the case that someone's training entailed greater than average personal sacrifice, we would agree that greater compensation was justified, just as we agree that if performing a job is more dangerous, unhealthy, tiring, or boring, and a society is organized so that someone must endure this while others have better work circumstances, a compensating wage differential is in order. But longer training time does not always connote greater personal sacrifice. Training always has a social opportunity cost, but we should not confuse the social opportunity cost with the private cost to the trainee, which is frequently far less. To the extent the scarce resources and time used in training are paid at "public expense," to the extent consumption opportunities are not diminished for those in training, and to the extent time spent in developing one's most socially productive talents is no more burdensome than time others spend training and working, training merits no compensation on equity grounds.

Which leaves us with Maxim 3. Whereas differences in contribution will be due to differences in talent, training, job assignment, luck, and effort, the only factor that deserves extra compensation is extra effort. If we define effort as personal sacrifice for the sake of the social endeavor, then only effort merits compensation. Of course, effort, as we define it, can take many forms. It may be longer work hours, less pleasant work, more intense, dangerous, or unhealthy work, and so on. It may consist of undergoing training that is less gratifying than the training experiences others enjoy. Below we examine arguments to the effect that difficulties in measuring effort, and the need to promote efficiency, may provide reasons for rewarding something other than effort. But our point here is that if reward were to be guided by equity considerations alone, compensation should be based on effort.

How can we concretely understand the difference between Maxims 2 and 3? According to *Amadeus,* Salieri was a dedicated, hard-working, but plodding composer, while Mozart was a frivolous, irresponsible genius. Assuming both could best serve the social interest by spending their work time as composers, then according to Maxim 2 Mozart deserved to be paid a great deal more than Salieri, while according to Maxim 3 Salieri deserved to be paid more than Mozart. So here we have a "test" of one's ethical inclinations. Would you pay Mozart or Salieri more? But remember, in judging equity you have to assume your answer will have no effect on the quantity or quality of either's compositions. And paying Salieri more does not mean you cannot choose to listen to Mozart!

Finally, before proceeding to the relation between equity and efficiency, we should clarify how a participatory, equitable economy will handle "free consumption." Even in economies that emphasize pecuniary calculations, individuals consume "free of charge" in some situations. That is, even in economies where solidarity is minimized, the public sometimes allows individuals to consume at "public expense" on the basis of need. Since we believe one of the merits of an equitable economy is that it creates the necessary conditions for a humane economy, and since we incorporate features designed to build solidarity in our allocative procedure, clearly we will expect considerable participatory consumption on the basis of need. This will occur in two different ways. First, particular consumption activities will be free to all individuals. This does not mean they have no social opportunity cost, or that they should be produced beyond the point where their social costs outweigh their social benefits. It simply means individuals will not be expected to reduce requests for other consumption activities because they consume more of these free goods. Students and sick people, for example, will not be expected to eat less. What items should be on the "free list" is something that will have to be debated and decided in consumer federations. Second, consumption will be on the basis of need when requests to that end are accepted by others in the economy. Frequently, individuals, or collectives, might propose a consumption request above the social average accompanied by an explanation of what they regard a justifiable need. These requests are considered on a discretionary basis and either approved by others or rejected. But there is no reason to suppose approvals will be infrequent.

Equity, Incentives, and Efficiency

Even among those who accept Maxim 3 as the only morally and logically defendable interpretation of equity, many think there is an unfortunate tradeoff between equity and efficiency, so that a reasonable system of rewards must strike a reasonable compromise.

It is surprising that this conviction is so commonplace, since the case for rewarding only effort on efficiency grounds *is more straightforward* than the case for rewarding only effort on equity grounds.

Once again, differences in outcome are due to differences in talent, training, job placement, luck, and effort. Once we clarify that "effort" includes personal sacrifices incurred in training, the only factor influencing performance over which an individual has any discretion is effort. By definition, neither talent nor luck can be induced by reward. Rewarding the occupant of a job for the contribution inherent in the job itself does not enhance performance. And provided that training is undertaken at public rather than private expense, no reward is required to induce people to seek training. In sum, if we include an effort component of training in our definition of effort, the only discretionary factor influencing performance is effort, and the only factor we should reward to enhance performance is effort.

This certainly turns common wisdom on its head! Not only is rewarding effort consistent with efficiency, but rewarding the combined effects of talent, training incurred at public not private expense, job placement, luck, and effort, is not. Suppose we wanted to induce maximum effort from runners in a 10,000-meter race. Should prize money be awarded according to place of finish, or according to improvements in personal best times? Rewarding outcome provides no incentive for poor runners with no chance of finishing "in the money" and no incentive for a clearly superior runner to run faster than necessary to finish first. Paying in accord with improvements in personal best times gives everyone an incentive to maximize her or his effort—if that is the kind of reward to which people respond. (We take up the issue of what constitutes effective "rewards" below.)

So why do many believe that equity conflicts with efficiency? There are three reasons cited that merit response.

1. If consumption opportunities are essentially equal, people will have no reason to work up to their capabilities.

In situations where solidarity is insufficient to elicit effort without reward, and where greater consumption opportunities are the only effective rewards, it will be inefficient to award equal consumption opportunities to those exerting unequal effort. But this is not what we have proposed. Below we challenge the facile equation of effective human rewards with differential consumption opportunities. But even so, we do not rule out correlating consumption opportunities with work effort. Our vision of consumption is that all should have a right to roughly equal consumption opportunities *because* our vision of production was that all should exert roughly equal effort in work. To the extent that job complexes are balanced so that no one is required to make greater personal work sacrifices than others, effort is equilibrated and therefore consumption should be as well.

But this is not to say that variations cannot be tolerated. Individual allocations of effort and consumption over time are perfectly acceptable. If someone wants to put in above average work effort now to consume above the social average later, or proposes to repay above average consumption now with more work effort later, this is perfectly acceptable. It means permitting individuals to equilibrate differential work efforts or consumption levels over time, and we see no reason to prevent individuals from "lending" and "borrowing" from their work mates whenever all concerned find it convenient. We also are not opposed to someone working less and consuming less over their lifetime, or to someone working extra hard or long in order to consume more. We personally believe the latter kind of variation can become unhealthy, but while we have described institutional structures that establish expectations that discourage excesses, and support informal social pressure against excesses, we do not

—51—

propose ruling out individual variations. No doubt people do have different preferences for income and leisure and there is no point legislating the same tradeoff for all. In any case, if the system we are describing has the kind of effect on people that we expect, people's attitudes toward work and what they find rewarding will evolve in ways that reduce current variations in work/leisure tradeoffs.

Thus, while we expect members of consumption councils to enjoy equal rights to consumption opportunities based on equal efforts exerted in their workers' councils, variations will exist and can be accounted for by a system of "report cards," if you will, that members receive from their workers' councils and bring to their consumption councils. The assessment could be a fully scaled effort rating—so many points above or below average. Or it could simply read "superior, average, or below average." Since circumstances and opinions will differ regarding the need and best means to calibrate effort, different workers' and consumers' councils will likely opt for different systems. But whatever differences in effort may arise, they will surely not lead to the extreme income differentials characterizing all economies today. And so the question finally arises, with no "sky to reach for," will people lift their arms?

In a society that makes every effort to depreciate the esteem that derives from anything other than conspicuous consumption, it is not surprising that great income differentials are seen as necessary to induce effort. But to assume that only conspicuous consumption can motivate people because under capitalism we have strained to make this so is unwarranted. There is plenty of evidence that people can be moved to great sacrifices for reasons other than a desire for personal wealth. Family members make sacrifices for one another without the slightest thought of material gain. Patriots die to defend their country's sovereignty. And there is good reason to believe that for nonpathological people wealth is generally coveted only as a *means* of attaining other ends such as economic security, comfort, social esteem, respect, status, or power.

We do not intend to debate the point at length, but if accumulating disproportionate consumption opportunities is often a means of achieving more fundamental rewards, as we believe, there is every reason to believe a powerful system of incentives need not be based on widely disparate consumption opportunities. If expertise and excellence are accorded social recognition directly, there will be no need to employ the intermediary device of conspicuous consumption. If economic security is guaranteed, as it will be in an equitable economy, there will be no need to accumulate out of fear for the future. If people participate in making decisions, as they will in a participatory economy, they will be more likely to carry out their responsibilities without recourse to external motivation. If the allocation of duties, responsibilities, sacrifices, and rewards is fair, and seen to be fair, as it will be in an equitable economy, sense of social duty will be a more powerful incentive than it is today. And if a fair share of effort and personal sacrifice are demanded by work mates who must otherwise pick up the slack, and if additional effort and sacrifice are appreciated by one's companions, recognized by society, and awarded commensurate increases in consumption opportunities, we are quite confident that incentives will be powerful indeed. The fact that there won't be motivation for excessive production to useless or egotistical ends would be a gain, not a loss.

2. If payment is equal, there is no incentive for people to train themselves in the ways they can be most socially valuable.

Since, presumably, Mozart could contribute more composing than engineering, it would have been inefficient had he studied engineering. And if Salieri would have made an even worse engineer than composer, the same follows for him. In general, it is efficient to develop the talents in which people have *comparative* advantages for reasons familiar to economists, which means incentives should facilitate rather than obstruct this outcome.

First, there is good reason to believe that people usually prefer to train in areas where they have more talent rather than less—unless there is a powerful incentive to do otherwise. Clearly there is no such disincentive in a participatory economic system. Those who could be composers, playwrights, musicians, and actors will not become lawyers, accountants, and insurance salespeople for "economic reasons." Nor will people in an equitable economy shun training that requires greater personal sacrifice since this component of effort will be fully compensated. Second, our system increases direct social recognition of excellence. In a participatory economy the best way to earn social esteem is to make notable contributions to others' well-being. Since this can best be done by training in accord with one's talents, there should be powerful incentives to do so. The only thing our system prohibits is paying ransoms to superstars. Instead we prefer to employ direct social recognition.

   3. Effort is difficult to measure while outcome is not, so reward-
      ing performance is the best system in practice.

Neither half of this proposition is as compelling as usually assumed. While economic textbooks speak blithely of marginal revenue products in infinite substitution models, the real world of social endeavors does not always cooperate. There are many situations where assigning responsibility for outcome is ambiguous. As those who have attempted to calibrate contributions to team performance can testify, there are some situations where it is easier than others. Sports teams are certainly more suited to such calibration than production teams. And it is more difficult to calibrate individual contribution in football and basketball than baseball. But even in baseball, arguably the easiest case of all, debates over different measures of offensive contribution, and acknowledgment of the importance of "intangibles" and "team chemistry," testify to the difficulty of assigning responsibility for outcomes.

Nor is measuring effort always so difficult. Anyone who has taught and graded students knows there are two different ways to proceed. One can compare students' performances to each other, or to an estimate of how well the student could have been expected to do. Admitting the possibility of grading according to "improvement" is tantamount to recognizing that teachers can, if they choose, measure effort. Given a student's level of preparation when she or he entered the class, given a student's natural ability, is this an A, B, or C effort, are not questions teachers, in general, find impossible to answer. It is also important to note who is responsible for measuring effort. Who is in a better position to know if someone is only giving the appearance of trying than the people working with her or him in the same kind of task? While teachers don't see student preparation, workers do see workmate's work. It is not as easy to pull the wool over the eyes of one's work mates as of one's supervisors.

Endogenous Preferences

In *Welfare Economics* we have written much on the subject of endogenous preferences, arguing that an endogenous view of preferences changes the assessment of the deficiencies of some well-known economic models. Here we briefly summarize the significance of endogenous preferences and what this implies for a participatory, equitable economy.

In traditional analysis, preferences are deemed exogenous. This means they do not alter due to specifically economic influences. Preferences may change due to schooling or aging but not due to our work or consumption. Most economists admit this is an abstraction. They realize that advertising has some effect and that people sometimes learn by consuming. But economists generally agree that abstracting from all this is more than justified by the resulting increase in clarity. Effects of endogenous factors are deemed minor, and if the examples most economists recognize were the only examples of endogenous preferences, we would not object too strenuously. But there is another way preferences are endogenous.

Just as people can account for the "preference fulfillment effect" of their consumption choices, they can also account for the "preference development effect," at least in some approximate way. If my future characteristics depend to some extent on what I do today, and if my preferences always depend in part on the characteristics I have, then my present consumption choices have preference development implications as well as preference fulfillment effects. Clearly, to the extent I can anticipate them, it would be irrational for me to ignore the preference development effects. In short, a strong incentive exists for people to develop preferences in accord with the anticipated terms of availability of different activities.

For example, it makes sense to develop preferences for consumption activities that are going to be easily available but not for activities that are unlikely to be available, or only available at great personal cost. For this reason, anticipated terms of availability for different consumption goods will exert an influence on people's preferences for those goods. While this complicates the logic of evaluating economic performance, it poses no welfare problems as long as there is no systematic bias in the terms of availability of different consumption activities. That is, as long as people are free to develop preferences in unbiased circumstances and as long as terms of availability are determined only by true social costs, the fact that people adjust preferences in accord with those social costs is perfectly consistent with efficiency. But, as we argued in *Welfare Economics*, market allocations are systematically biased against provision of public goods and goods with greater than average positive external effects, and hierarchical production relations and central planning are both systematically biased against self-managed work opportunities. Moreover, these biases are pervasive and significant rather than trivial, and individually rational adjustments to them prove socially counterproductive in the sense that when individuals adjust, the biases grow over time, thereby generating ever greater losses of potential well-being.

So, the question is whether any features of our model of a participatory, equitable economy bias the terms of availability of different kinds of human activities. We designed the system for organizing production precisely to avoid biases against participation and self-management. Likewise, the system of nested federations of consumers' councils and the method of charging people for collective goods avoids the antipublic bias inherent in market allocations. But whether there are any counterproductive biases present in the allocative procedures we propose is best discussed after describing our planning procedure and investigating its welfare properties, to which we now turn.

4

ALLOCATION

[I]t is clear that someone (some institution) has to tell the producer about what the users require. If that 'someone' is not the impersonal market mechanism it can only be a hierarchical superior. There are horizontal links (market), there are vertical links (hierarchy). What other dimension is there? ...In a complex industrial economy the interrelation between its parts can be based in principle either on freely chosen negotiated contracts (which means autonomy and a species of commodity production) or on a system of binding instructions from planning offices. There is no third way.

—*Alec Nove*

Necessity is the argument of tyrants. It is the creed of slaves.
—*William Pitt Jr.*

In this chapter we describe an alternative system of allocation, which we call decentralized participatory planning. The system permits consumers' and workers' councils to participate directly in formulating a plan and has strong egalitarian properties. Because workers' and consumers' councils propose and revise their own activities prior to initiating those activities, the planning process is a decentralized, social, iterative procedure.

We consider specifying this procedure and analyzing its welfare theoretic properties our most important contribution to developing a libertarian egalitarian economic vision. The idea of "associated producers" democratically determining their own plan is no more original to us than the vision of workers' and consumers' councils. But whereas many before us have contributed to the theory of the internal workings of democratic councils, few have attempted to explain, in detail, how those councils might jointly settle on a plan.[1] In fact, most economists agree that no third procedure qualitatively different from markets and central planning exists, or, if there is another alternative, that it has not been articulated at a level permitting meaningful comparison with markets and central planning.

Alec Nove, for example, threw down the gauntlet in unequivocal terms: "I feel increasingly ill-disposed towards those who...substitute for hard thinking an image of a world in which there would be no economic problems at all (or where any problems that might arise would be handled smoothly by the 'associated producers'.... In a complex industrial economy the interrelation between its parts can be based in principle either on freely chosen negotiated contracts [i.e., markets], or on a system of binding instructions from planning offices [i.e., central planning]. There is no third way."[2]

Allen Buchanan posed the challenge in a somewhat more agnostic vein: "It is impossible to show that a feasible nonmarket system at least approaches the productivity of the market unless (1) a rather well-developed theoretical model of the nonmarket system is available, and (2) it is demonstrated that a sufficiently productive approximation of the ideal...system described in the theoretical model is practically possible. Unfortunately, [no one] has achieved even the first step—that of providing a theoretical model for a nonmarket system."[3]

In this chapter and the next two we present a rebuttal to Nove and a direct answer to Buchanan by providing a "rather well-developed" theoretical model of a decentralized planning procedure and offering a preliminary analysis of its efficiency properties as well as arguing that a "sufficiently productive approximation of the ideal...system

---

1. One recent exception is Pat Devine who presents a model of "democratic planning" in part IV of *Democracy and Economic Planning* (Boulder, Colo.: Westview Press, 1988).

2. Alec Nove, *The Economics of Feasible Socialism* (London: George Allen and Unwin, 1983), ix-x, 44.

3. Allen Buchanan, *Ethics, Efficiency, and the Market* (Totowa, N.J.: Rowman and Littlefield, 1985), 29.

described in the theoretical model is practically possible," including description of a number of experiments through which other economists might sensibly test this claim.

Participatory Information and Communication

Our description of participatory workers' and consumers' councils assumed that the necessary information about their relations with others would be available. But what precisely do workers in a council need to know to regulate their production activity cognizant of the effects on themselves, other workers, and consumers? And what must consumers know to formulate their consumption requests in light of their own needs as well as the needs of other consumers and workers?

Participatory workers must be able to weigh the gains from working less or employing less productive though more fulfilling techniques, against the consequent loss of consumer well-being. Participatory consumers need to be able to weigh the gains of a consumption request against the sacrifices required to produce it. Participatory workers must be able to distinguish an equitable work load from one that is too light or too heavy. And participatory consumers need to be able to distinguish reasonable consumption demands from ones that are unreasonable or overly modest. Finally, all actors must know the true social costs and benefits of things they demand or supply, that is, all the nonhuman and human, quantifiable and nonquantifiable consequences of their choices, if they are going to participate in informed collective self-management.

First Communicative Tool: Prices

Prices providing accurate estimates of the full social costs and benefits of inputs and outputs are the most important quantitative communicative tools we use. They arise in the process of participatory planning and serve as guides to proposals and evaluations. And this is an important point. All too often theoretical economists view "efficiency" prices or "shadow" prices as quantitative measures that can be found via technical procedures. In the literature on central planning, for example, shadow prices arise as the solution to the dual of the primal planning problem that central planners "solve." And in neoclassical literature on market systems, an equilibrium price vector is studied as something implied by preferences and technologies taken as givens. While these conceptions are useful in some regards, they are misleading as well. Real people's preferences arise in social communicative processes. Not only do results depend on what those processes are like, but the very preferences that lie at the basis of the results depend on the processes as well. So, without engaging in undue mystification, we should remember that estimates of social costs and benefits with any claim to accuracy must arise from social, communicative processes. The trick is to organize these processes so people have no incentives to dissimulate regarding their true desires, and all have equal opportunity to manifest their feelings. It is precisely because our participatory planning process is different from the flawed communicative processes of market and centrally planned allocation that the prices to which it gives rise will be different as well.

In any case, prices are "indicative" during the planning process in the sense of indicating the best current estimates of final valuations. They are not binding but flexible in the sense that qualitative information provides important additional guidance. And they are not the product of competition or authoritarian determinations, but of social consultation and compromise. The idea is that qualitative information is necessary if quantitative indicators are to be kept as accurate as possible. But qualitative information is also necessary to develop workers' sensitivity to fellow workers' situations and everyone's understanding of the intricate tapestry of human relations that determines what we can and cannot consume or produce. So both to assure accuracy and to foster solidarity we need a continual, social resetting of prices in light of updated qualitative information about work lives and consumption activity. Thus, the cybernetic burden of a participatory allocation procedure is considerably greater than for nonparticipatory economies. Not only must a participatory economy generate and revise accurate quantitative measures of social costs and benefits in light of changing conditions, but it must communicate substantial qualitative information about others' conditions as well.

Second Communicative Tool: Measures of Work

As we explained in chapter 2, job complexes are balanced in each workplace, and in plants with above average work conditions workers spend time doing more menial tasks elsewhere, while in plants with below average work conditions, people put time into more interesting pursuits elsewhere.

For an individual to work more or less than the social average in a given period and not disrupt a humane balance of work, she or he need only diminish or increase her or his hours worked at all tasks in the same proportion. Then, each individual could receive from her or his workplace an indicator of average labor hours expended as an accurate indicator of work contributed. Over a sufficient period, whenever a person's indicator was high (or low) compared to the social average, the individual would have sacrificed more (or less) for the social good, and would be entitled to ask for proportionately more (or less) consumption in return. Unlike what emerges from the marxist labor theory of value: (1) In our system job complexes are balanced by a real social evaluation, and (2) our "hour counts" serve only as guidelines for decisions since councils can grant exceptions for higher (or lower) consumption requests as conditions and needs warrant.

In short, participatory planning can obtain a reasonable first estimate of effort expended by counting labor hours because people's job complexes have been balanced. These estimates can then be revised in light of effort intensity ratings by one's work mates. In attempting to gain consumption flexibility, only unbalancing job complexes is prohibited.

Third Communicative Tool: Qualitative Activity

To guard against "reductionist accounting" each actor needs access to a list of everything that goes into producing goods directly and indirectly, and a description of what will be gained from consuming them. This means those who produce and consume particular goods must try to communicate the qualitative human effects that cannot be captured in quantitative indicators. This does not entail everyone writing Upton Sinclair length novels about their work and living conditions. It does mean generating concise accounts that substitute for the fact that not everyone can personally experience every circumstance. Of course, not every worker and consumer will use all this qualitative information in all calculations. But over time people will become familiar with the "congealed" material, human, and social components of products they use just as people are now familiar with the products themselves. In this way, everyone can more accurately assess the full effects of others' requests in a way that enhances solidarity. Both producers and consumers must therefore receive not only quantitative summaries of overall social costs and benefits, but detailed qualitative accounts as well. Only this will ensure that the human/social dimension of economic decision making is not lost and guarantee that summary price data remains as accurate as possible.

Allocation Organization

Every workplace and neighborhood consumers' council participates in the social, iterative procedure we call participatory planning. But besides workplace councils, we also have industry councils and regional federations of workers' councils. And besides neighborhood consumers' councils, we also have ward, city, county, and state federations of consumers' councils as well as a national consumers' council. Moreover, in addition to all these councils and federations of councils, various facilitation boards assess collective proposals and large-scale investment projects, regional and industry boards assist workers changing places of employment, and household boards help individuals and families find membership in living units and neighborhoods. Finally, at every level of the economy facilitation boards help units revise proposals and search out the least disruptive ways of modifying plans in response to unforeseen circumstances.

In our companion volume, *Looking Forward*, we provide comprehensive descriptions of planning institutions and procedures, including hypothetical case studies for particular kinds of workplaces and consumers' councils intended to illustrate the texture of participatory planning. Here we present a summary of results sufficient for theoretical purposes.

Participatory Planning

Each consumption "actor" proposes a consumption plan. Individuals make proposals for private goods. Neighborhood councils make proposals that include approved requests for private goods as well as the neighborhood's collective consumption request. Higher level federations make proposals that include approved requests from member councils as well as the federation's collective consumption request.

Similarly, each production "actor" proposes a production plan. Workplaces enumerate the inputs they want and outputs they will make available. Regional and industry federations aggregate proposals and keep track of excess supply and demand. Every actor at every level proposes its own plan, and, after receiving information regarding other actors' proposals and the response of other actors to its proposal, each actor makes a new proposal. As every actor "bargains" through successive "iterations," the process converges.

Preparing First Proposals

The real world always has a "just completed year." If production and consumption of the just completed year was recorded, we would have information about last year's plan for each actor. If the prices used to calculate social costs, benefits, and income last year were recorded, we have a set of "indicative prices" that could be used to begin this year's estimates as well. By storing last year's full plan in a central computer, access to relevant parts including indicative prices could be made available to all actors in the planning process. Additionally, each unit knows what its own proposals were in each iteration last year.

So, how do workers' and consumers' councils plan?

1. They access relevant data from last year.

2. They receive information from facilitation boards estimating this year's probable changes in prices and income in light of existing knowledge of past investment decisions and changes in the labor force.

3. They receive information from higher level production and consumption councils regarding long-term investment

projects or collective consumption proposals already agreed to in previous plans that imply commitments for this year.

4. By reviewing changes in their own proposals made during last year's planning they assess how much they had to scale down their consumption desires or their plans to improve the quality of work life, and look to see what increases in average income and improvements in the quality of average work complexes are projected this year over last.

5. Using last year's final prices as indicators of social costs and benefits they develop a proposal for the coming year, not only enumerating what they want to consume or produce— and implicitly what they think society's total output should be—but also providing qualitative information about their reasons.

This does not mean units must specify how many units of every single good they need down to size, style, and color. Goods and services are grouped into classes accordingly as they are roughly interchangeable regarding the resources, intermediate goods, and labor required to make them. For planning purposes we need only request types, even though later everyone will pick an exact size, style, and color. Individuals present consumption requests to neighborhood councils where they are approved or disapproved. Once approved, individual consumption requests are summed and added to the neighborhood collective consumption request to become the neighborhood consumption proposal. These in turn are summed with consumption requests from other neighborhoods into ward proposals, which are summed along with consumption requests from other wards into city proposals. Having the next higher level council review, approve, or contest lower level requests until they are ready to be passed on saves a great deal of planning time.

In the same way, a firm's iteration board provides all its workers with summaries of last year's production schedule, including what was initially proposed, changes made during planning iterations, and what was (finally) approved, as well as a prediction of this year's requests based on extrapolations from new demographic data and the trajectory of last year's iterations. Individual workers consider this information, discuss ideas for improving the quality of work life, and enter proposals which are averaged into the firm's first proposal for "inputs" and "outputs." After some number of iterations, firm proposals are discussed, negotiated, and decided as a unit rather than each individual making his or her own proposal and these being averaged.

Besides quantitative proposals for each production and consumption unit, a qualitative addenda including descriptions of changes in circumstances and conditions is also entered into the computerized planning system. At any point any council can access the data banks of any facilitation board and any other council.

Proceeding from One Proposal to Another

The first proposals are in. We have all answered how much we want to work and consume in light of our own presumably over-optimistic assessments of possibilities. Do the proposals constitute a plan, or must we have another round? To decide, it is only necessary to sum all proposals and compare total demand and total supply for every class of final good and service, intermediate good, and primary input. In a first iteration, where consumers propose in part a "wish list" and workers propose substantial improvements in their work lives, while some goods may be in excess supply, for most goods initial proposals should generate excess demand. In other words, initial proposals are not supposed to sum to a feasible plan. As the next step, every council receives new information indicating which goods are in excess supply or demand by what percentage, and how its proposal compares to those of other relevant units. Most important, iteration boards provide new estimates of indicative prices projected to equilibrate supply and demand.

At this point, consumers reassess their requests in light of the new prices and most often "shift" their requests for goods in excess demand toward goods whose relative prices have fallen because they were in excess supply or less in excess demand than others. Consumers' councils whose overall requests were higher than average would also be under pressure to "whittle down" their requests in hopes of winning approval. Equity and efficiency emerge simultaneously. The need to win approval from other similar councils forces councils whose per capita consumption request is significantly above the social average to reduce their overall requests. But the need to reduce can be alleviated by substituting goods whose indicative prices have fallen for those whose prices have risen. Attention focuses on the degree to which units diverge from current and projected averages, and on whether their reasons for doing so are compelling.

Similarly workers' councils whose ratios of social benefits of outputs to social costs of inputs were lower than average would come under pressure to increase either efficiency or effort, or to explain why the quantitative indicators are misleading in their particular case. Before increasing their work commitment, workers would try to substitute inputs whose indicative prices had fallen for inputs whose indicative prices had risen, and substitute outputs whose indicative prices had risen for outputs whose indicative prices had fallen.

Each iteration yields a new set of proposed activities for all economic actors. Once summed, these yield new data regarding the status of each good and the average consumption per person and production "benefit cost ratio" per firm. All this allows calculation of new price projections and new predictions for average income and work, which in turn lead to modifications in proposals until excess demands are eliminated and a feasible plan is reached.

Flexible Updating

Converging and updating are related because both can benefit from algorithms that take advantage of the large scale of the planning process. Assume we have settled on a plan for the year. Why might we need to update it during the year, and how might this be done with least disruption?

Consumers begin the year with a working plan including how much of different kinds of food, clothing, meals at restaurants, trips, books, records, and tickets to performances they will consume. What if someone wants to substitute one item for a slightly different one? Or what if she wants to delete or add entries? Or what if she changes her mind and wants to save or borrow more than planned? She belongs to a neighborhood consumers' council which in turn belongs to a ward council, a city federation, and so on. Some changes will cancel out among all the consumers within the neighborhood, others will cancel out at the ward level, and so on. As long as adjustments by many consumers cancel at some consumption federation level, production plans need not change. Indeed, making adjustments without disrupting production plans is one function of consumer federation boards.

But what happens if aggregate demand rises for some good? Suppose individuals record their consumption on "credit card" computers that automatically compare the percentage of annual requests "drawn down" with the fraction of the year that has passed, taking account of predictable irregularities such as birth dates and holidays. This data can be processed by planning terminals which communicate projected changes to relevant industry councils which in turn communicate changes to particular firms. The "technology" involved is little different from the now common system of computerized store inventories where cash register sales are automatically subtracted from inventory stocks. In any case, what would then happen is that consumer federations, industry councils, and individual work units would engage in a dialog to negotiate adjustments. Such dialogues may lead to work diminishing in some industries and increasing in others, including possible transfers of employees, but there need be no more moving about than in other types of economies. In any case, the need for workers to change jobs or increase or diminish work loads would be a factor considered in the dialogue over whether to meet changed demands.

However, since each firm's activities have implications for other firms, if planned matches between supply and demand are calculated too closely, any change in demand could disrupt the whole economy. For this reason a "taut" plan would prove unnecessarily inconvenient since it would require excessive debating and moving. To avoid this and to simplify updating, the plan agreed to should include some excess supply for most goods. A practical knowledge of those industries most likely to be affected by nonaveraging alterations would facilitate this type of "slack planning."

Converging to a Plan

A little thought reveals that convergence can be a complicated matter. Adjusting indicative prices to reduce excess supplies and demands is more complicated in practice than in economists' theoretical models with all their convenient assumptions. For example, a product in excess demand in one iteration could overshoot equilibrium and be in excess supply in the next iteration as workers offer to produce more and consumers offer to request less in response to a price increase. Worse still, considering that each product's status affects the status of many others, progress in one industry could disrupt equilibrium in another. Theoreticians' solutions to these headaches always assume away the troublesome phenomena. Whether the issue is market equilibrium and stability or convergence of iterative planning procedures, it is well known that convexity and gross substitutability assumptions are good aspirin for these theoretical headaches. But simplifying assumptions are no aspirin at all for practitioners operating in the real world.

To make our participatory planning procedure more efficient, specific economies will incorporate flexible rules that facilitate convergence in a reasonable time but do not unduly bias outcomes or subvert equity. Procedures can range from rote algorithms carried out by computer that take short cuts toward equilibrium, to rules that prohibit actors' responses that would yield time consuming loops, to adjustments fashioned and implemented by specialized workers experienced in facilitating convergence when particular situations arise. Devising and choosing from among these and other possibilities is a practical issue in implementing any actual participatory economy. Assuming the procedures chosen do not violate principles essential to participatory planning, considerations include (1) the extent to which iteration workers could bias outcomes, (2) the extent of reductions in the number of iterations required to reach a plan, (3) the amount of planning time saved through compartmentalizing subsets of iterations, and (4) how much less onerous to producers and consumers their calculations could be made.

A Typical Planning Process

Since the procedure we have described is dramatically different from traditional market and central planning allocation, it is useful to summarize by describing what a typical planning process might look and feel like to its participants.

The first step is for each individual to think about her or his plan for the year. Individuals know they will end up working in a balanced job complex, and can expect to consume an average consumption bundle unless their work effort is above or below normal or special needs dictate otherwise. The first decision is whether they want to "save" by working longer or consuming less than average, or "borrow" by working less or consuming more than average. Facilitation boards provide an initial estimate of what average consumption and average work loads will be for the year based on last year's levels, last year's investments in equipment and training, and adjustments that occurred during last year's iterations. When you make your first proposal you are not only proposing to do specific work and consume specific items, but you are proposing a level of work contribution and consumption request for yourself, and, implicitly, at least on average, for everyone else as well. To be realistic you must coordinate your work and consumption proposals, though you need not agree with facilitation board growth estimates.

In other words, what you propose is: "I would like to work so much at my job complex and to consume so much broken down in the following way." And this proposal is based on last year's experience, your prediction of economic growth, and your individual decision about saving and borrowing. Everyone makes such a choice, trying to optimize given their particular preferences and within the constraint that the overall amount consumed must be produced and that responsibilities and rewards in this endeavor will be distributed equitably.

After first proposals are summed, new indicative prices are calculated and new projections of social averages estimated. Note that it would not even be possible to implement most initial production proposals since in most firms one person in a team may have proposed working more hours than another person in the same team, even though they can only work together. Moreover, most goods will be in excess demand so the initial plan is infeasible as well.

Again every individual would formulate a new response. You compare your proposed work load and proposed consumption to the average proposals of others. You might also consider more localized averages, for example in your firm or industry, and in your council or neighborhood. You certainly consider the status of each item you ordered or proposed since excess demands and supplies will be reflected in changes in indicative prices. That is, you will be faced with summaries of the statuses of goods as well as new estimates of social opportunity costs and benefits. After you consult descriptive explanations for what seems odd to you, like large changes in worker productivity or consumer choice, and after you consult with whomever you like and whatever data you are interested in, you then make any desired changes before entering your second proposals.

And, once again, all these new proposals are summed and the new information made available for the third iteration. So far there have been no rules or limits on workers' or consumers' responses. Now, however, there could be a change. Instead of being able to change proposals in any direction by any amount, limits might be imposed. For example, consumers might be prohibited from increasing their demand for certain goods beyond some maximum percentage above projected averages for the economy. Or producers might be prevented from lowering output proposals by more than some percent in this and subsequent rounds.

The point is simply that it is possible to impose rules limiting changes to specific ranges to keep the status of goods from varying excessively from round to round. Any particular implementation of participatory planning settles on socially desirable and mechanically efficient rules to guide the behavior of producers and consumers in different iterations.

In the third or fourth iteration, proposals might be limited to councils instead of individuals. Consumers meet in their local neighborhood councils and workers in their workplace councils to settle on councilwide proposals so that work proposals are no longer abstract unimplementable averages but consistent work plans that could be enacted if inputs requested were made available.

Note that nothing about our procedures pushes different actors to consume the same amounts of different goods. Individual consumers and producers can hold pat on proposals that are far from average. On the other hand, workplaces do feel pressure to measure up to average "benefit cost ratios," and consumers will be pressured to keep their overall requests from exceeding average income. Indeed, at this stage production councils that persist, after allowance for acknowledged different circumstances, in proposals with benefit cost ratios below their industry's average, might have to petition their industry for permission not to be disbanded. And, similarly, although again with sensible allowances, local consumers' councils with above average proposals might have to petition higher federations explaining special circumstances to warrant their requests.

The fifth iteration in our hypothetical procedure might deploy still another rule to accelerate planning. This time facilitation boards extrapolate from the previous iterations to provide five different final plans that could be reached by the iterative process. What distinguishes the five plans is that each entails slightly different total product, work expended, average consumption, and average investment. All actors then vote, as units, for one of these five feasible plans. Each plan is a consistent whole and implementable. Once one of the five is chosen as the base operating plan, units adjust requests in subsequent iterations in conformity with the base plan until individual agreements are also reached.

Conclusion

While we must still address important aspects of participatory allocation in chapter 5, it is useful to summarize here where our argument stands. In chapter 1 we argued that hierarchical production and consumption, markets, and central planning were individually and in combination incompatible with efficient, egalitarian, economies in which people control their own lives and enjoy solidarity. In chapter 2 we presented a description of participatory, nonhierarchical production. In chapter 3 we added a description of participatory, equitable consumption. In this chapter we have described a planning procedure that promotes participation, equity, solidarity, and variety and supports rather than undermines participatory production and consumption within units.

What remains is to demonstrate that a participatory economy can yield desirable outcomes efficiently. To do that we examine the convergence and efficiency properties of a mathematical model of participatory planning in chapter 5, and propose various simulation and other social experiments regarding its "practical feasibility" in chapter 6.

5

WELFARE

Annual income twenty pounds, annual expenditure nineteen pounds nineteen and six, result happiness. Annual income twenty pounds, annual expenditure twenty pounds ought and six, result misery.

—Charles Dickens

It is impossible to show that a feasible nonmarket system at least approaches the productivity of the market unless a rather well developed theoretical model of the nonmarket system is available.

—Allen Buchanan

In this chapter we present a formal model of participatory planning to compare its convergence and efficiency properties with those of formal models of market and centrally planned economies. We show that:

1. A formal model of participatory planning can attain optimal outcomes under less restrictive assumptions than necessary for formal models of market and centrally planned economies.

2. While there is good reason to believe that real world versions of market and centrally planned models will perform less efficiently than analyses of their formal models predict, there is good reason to believe that real world versions of participatory planning would perform better than their

formal model predicts. Realistic markets and central planning aggravate their formal model's failures. Realistic participatory planning reduces its formal model's failures.

Preliminary Insights

In the previous three chapters we described participatory production, consumption, and allocation. For production and consumption we argued that participation and equity were compatible with efficiency. To answer this question for allocation, we now construct a formal model of participatory planning.

However, formal models of economic systems in many cases have been misleading. Typically, a model is presented based on various assumptions. Interpreters then draw conclusions about real economic systems or make policy recommendations. But this permits two kinds of deception: (1) Since only some aspects of an economic system will be represented in the formal model, unrepresented aspects may yield different actual results than those derived in the formal model; and (2) since conclusions derived from the formal model depend on particular assumptions, if an explicit assumption does not hold in real conditions, actual results may diverge from those derived from the model. To avoid deceiving ourselves we distinguish between the full version of a participatory economy we have described in previous chapters (hereafter PE), and the Formal Model of a participatory economy we construct below (hereafter FMPE). We specify which aspects of PE are incorporated in FMPE and which are not. And we specify exactly which assumptions underpin the conclusions we draw from FMPE. This allows us to compare results from our formal model with results from formal models of traditional economic systems, and to evaluate the reasonableness of drawing real world conclusions from the formal models.

Differences Between PE and FMPE

Interpersonal Empathy

Interpersonal empathy exists if my level of fulfillment depends in part on other's fulfillment, for example, if I feel better when others feel better. We believe this kind of interpersonal empathy exists—my welfare varies directly with other people's welfare—even under adverse circumstances and can become an important factor under favorable circumstances. Since PE is designed to promote this sentiment, our description of PE incorporated features based on interpersonal empathy. But we do not assume interpersonal empathy in FMPE and do not include features such as the exchange of qualitative information about concrete situations discussed in FMPE. We exclude these features both because they are difficult to model formally, and, more important, so we can see what conclusions can be derived even if actors in the economy had no interpersonal empathy. Specifically, we want to demonstrate that convergence and optimality results for participatory planning do not depend on the existence of empathy among participants.

Global Motivations

A second difference arises because in PE each consumer knows that she or he is also a worker. The quality of someone's work life depends on the overall demand for goods and services, which depends on per capita consumption, which is implicit in each individual's consumption proposal. Thus, global interactions in PE provide additional motives for its citizens to make socially responsible work and consumption proposals. In PE, each actor considers total welfare which includes preference fulfillment and preference development effects resulting from both her or his consumption and production activities. Moreover, the participatory actor understands that under equitable conditions it is in every individual's interest to maximize over all social well being given the productive skills, equipment, and resources available. This is why PE's actors will know, for example, that in the (not so) long run they have more to gain from investments that greatly improve the quality of work life in other people's workplaces than from investments that only slightly improve the quality of work life in their own workplace. If investment raises work quality locally, PE eventually distributes the benefits to all.

In FMPE, however, we assume people maximize as consumers and workers independently and can "capture" local improvements within the leeway permitted by specific constraints. Again, the reasons are ease of modeling and demonstrating that particular conclusions do not rely on assuming that people have what some may regard as "an advanced state of consciousness."

Levels of Involvement

FMPE contains only neighborhood and workers' councils so that none of the federations of consumers' councils or of regional and industry workers' councils are modeled explicitly in FMPE. As we explained earlier, organizing consumption in nested federations helps create an "incentive compatible" system of expressing preferences for public goods. Similarly, regional federations of workers' councils help to efficiently resolve "production externalities," and industry federations can deal with economies of scale. Since the reason for creating FMPE is to test the efficiency properties of PE, one might question deleting federations from the formal model. The answer is that they are not included explicitly because they do not have to be, as we will see. But this is not to say they are not critical features for ensuring efficiency in PE.

Facilitation Procedures

In PE we allowed for behavioral rules that would limit the range of responses of actors and facilitate price adjustments as the iterations proceed. In contrast, FMPE assumes nondiscretionary, arbitrary percentage adjustments. Although the discretionary rules in PE are themselves somewhat arbitrary and chosen only to hasten convergence with minimal disruption of efficiency and equity, their presence nonetheless constitutes a difference we need to bear in mind.

Available Information

Arguably the most dramatic difference between FMPE and PE is the widespread use of qualitative information in the latter. The fact that consumers and producers in PE have access to detailed descriptions of how people work and consume, and the effects of each, allows actors' economic involvements to be more "human" than in any system entirely dependent on quantitative prices. Again, ease of modeling and a desire to test if particular conclusions hinge on this information dictate deleting qualitative information from FMPE.

Summary of Differences

In sum:

1. FMPE does not account for interpersonal empathy.

2. FMPE does not account for "global" awareness.

3. FMPE does not explicitly define federations of consumption or production councils, although FMPE can be interpreted so as to incorporate their effects.

4. FMPE contains no special convergence hastening procedures.

5. FMPE has less robust informational features.

At various points in this chapter, we will return to these differences to assess whether results for FMPE should also apply to PE.

Modeling Consumption

In PE consumers councils make proposals that maximize their members' well-being and development without presuming preferential treatment for themselves, or, in other words, subject to the constraint that all other consumers have equal opportunity to do so as well.[1]

More specifically, each consumers' council maximizes its own members' well-being and development subject to the constraint that it should not presume to use more of society's scarce productive resources and sometimes debilitating labor efforts per member than any other council, unless special dispensation is given.

To model consumption behavior in FMPE we remember, therefore, that consumers in local PE councils collectively develop a request for goods, taking into account effects on their immediate well being and on their developmental capacities, which together constitute their total economic well being. Let $W(h)$ represent the total economic well being of consmers' council $CC(h)$ as evidenced by their collective requests. Let $U(h)$ represent the immediate well-

---

1. We assume for convenience equal work efforts and no borrowing or lending. Any divergences would be accounted for as explained in chapter 3.

being of consumers' council CC(h). Let C(h) be the vector of the human characteristics of CC(h)'s members which define the abilities of the members of CC(h) to garner well-being from engaging in various consumption activities. Let the changes in human characteristics of the people in council CC(h) be ΔC(h), and note that the motivation for desiring a particular ΔC(h) will be to arrive at more favorable C(h) from which to derive well-being in the future.[1]

Then the welfare that a consumers' council seeks to maximize in its consumption planning efforts is:

$$W(h) = W(U(h), \Delta C(h))$$

Now let:

x be a vector of production activity levels

A be the input matrix of produced goods for those activities (intermediate inputs)

K be the capital input coefficient matrix (machines and plant capacity that must be on hand to produce outputs)

$k*$ be the vector of available capital goods

R be the input matrix of nonproducible, scarce resources

$r*$ be the vector of available, nonproducible, scarce resources

L be the direct labor input matrix of different kinds of labor

$l*$ be the vector of available labor inputs

v be a (row) vector of relative social values of produced goods

So $\{A, K, R, L\}$ constitute the technical relations of production in the economy and include multiple techniques. But we assume for now that each activity produces a single output so we can identify industries by the goods they produce.

An elementary result is that if p_k is the vector of shadow prices for scarce capital goods, p_r is the vector of shadow prices for scarce

---

1. This unconventional treatment of preference fulfillment and development as components of total economic well being is further elaborated in chapter 6 of *Welfare Economics*.

nonproductive resources, and p_l is the vector of shadow prices for different types of labor, the vector (p_k, p_r, p_l) is the solution to the dual of the primal programming problem for the entire economy. The primal problem would be:

$$\text{Primal: maximize } v(I - A)x$$

$$\text{s.t. } Kx \leq k*, \quad Rx \leq r*, \quad Lx \leq l*, \quad \text{and } x \geq 0$$

And the dual problem would be:

$$\text{Dual: minimize } (p_k k* + p_r r* + p_l l*)$$

$$\text{s.t. } p_k K + p_r R + p_l L \geq v(1 - A),$$

$$p_k \geq 0, \quad p_r \geq 0, \text{ and } p_l \geq 0$$

Where the dual constraint can also be written

$$\{ p_k K + p_r R + p_l L \}(I - A)^{-1} \geq v$$

which simply says that shadow prices must be such that the value of all the resources and labor used both directly and indirectly in any activity engaged in, plus the value of all the capital goods committed to the activity both directly and indirectly, must be at least as great as the social benefit from the activity.

Now, suppose $\hat{y}_h$ is a vector of particular quantities of different kinds of produced goods requested by council CC(h). Then

$$\{ p_k K + p_r R + p_l L \}(I - A)^{-1}\hat{y}_h$$

would be the quantifiable social cost of consumption proposal $\hat{y}_h$.

We should note that if the shadow prices for labor were derived from the solution to the dual programming problem, as stated, then while they would reflect the different productivities of different kinds of work—the result of labor supplies, technological possibilities, and preferences for goods—they would not reflect differential desirabilities from the workers' point of view. In which case the above equation would not be a completely accurate indicator of the social cost of a consumption proposal. However, the shadow prices for labor generated by the iterative planning procedure we describe below for FMPE *do* include this component. And since the shadow prices we use are those derived from the FMPE procedure defined below, not the shadow prices from the dual programmming problem discussed in this heuristic explanation of the problems faced by consumer and producer actors in our economy, the estimates of social costs we calculate in FMPE *do* reflect the differential desirabilities of different categories of work.

This heuristic presentation is sufficient to illustrate the logic of consumption. Consumers in CC(h) propose bundles they like considering both the preference fulfillment effect and the changes they expect their consumption activity to produce. That is, consumers seek to maximize their own total economic well-being, W(h), where

$$W(h) = W(U(h), \Delta C(h))$$

But consumption proposals will be judged by other consumers according to whether they imply a greater than per capita use of scarce productive resources, machinery, and laboring capabilities. That is, others will want to know if

$$\left\{ p_k K + p_r R + p_l L \right\} (I - A)^{-1} [\hat{y}_h - \hat{y}_a]$$

is greater than, less than, or equal to zero, where $\hat{y}_a$ is the average consumption bundle requested by the H consumption councils in the economy which, for convenience, we assume have the same number of members.

$$\hat{y}_a = \sum_h \frac{\hat{y}_h}{H}$$

In PE, consumers are invited to critically assess each others' proposals, and in particular others might comment regarding what kind of $\Delta C(h)$ are being sought. But for proposals that do not exceed average social cost per consumer, other councils can only advise not veto. On the other hand, for proposals in excess of average social cost per consumer, other consumers' councils are permitted veto powers. To model this we assume that the above inequality operates as a constraint faced by consumers' council CC(h) in FMPE.

Differences from Participatory Consumption

As we noted earlier, this model deviates from participatory consumption in some respects.

1. To correspond to the consumption side of a real participatory economy, the model would have to explicitly include individuals.

The absence of individuals is a minor difference that can be handled in two ways. We could confine each unit in FMPE to one member. Or, more realistically, we can note that if the council FMPE model yields desirable results, nothing precludes the individuals in each unit from dispersing the group's "bounty" among themselves efficiently and fairly.

2. There is a difference regarding consumers' presumed goals. In FMPE consumers try to maximize their own well-being and development without including as one of their goals the well-being of people in other units.

To be sure, FMPE's consumption constraint ensures that equity is preserved, but it incorporates no institutional or motivational sensitivity to how the well-being of some depends on the well-being of others. Actors in PE, on the other hand, are capable of expressing and developing solidarity. This difference, however, does not mean PE will not perform as well as FMPE.

3. FMPE includes no mechanism for communication or use of qualitative data.

While a significant difference, again this does not diminish the likelihood that PE will perform as well as FMPE.

4. The absence of explicitly defined federations of consumers in FMPE appears to be a significant difference from PE that would certainly impact on the efficiency properties of FMPE.

However, FMPE is sufficiently abstract so that if and when it suits our purposes we can interpret any of the abstract consumers' councils in FMPE as a ward, city, state, or national federation of consumers' councils.

In other words, CC(h) may be a neighborhood consumer council, but CC(w) can be interpreted as a ward council, CC(s) as a state federation, and CC(n) as the national federation. So as long as it is clear that consumption federations participate as actors in the iterative planning process just as neighborhood consumers' councils do, that well-being functions for federations represent the average preferences for public goods of all members of a federation, and that consumers are "charged" their proportionate share of federation requests, FMPE is sufficient to "test" PE with regard to efficiency even under assumptions of public goods and external effects, as will become clear.

Modeling Production

Traditional economic theory treats work units as places where physical materials are transformed via an unspecified process employing human labor. The only concern is whether the transformation occurs efficiently. Could inputs be used to generate more outputs? Could we achieve the same physical transformations with less or less disagreeable labor?

In contrast, we view a workers' council, WC(j), as another center of human activity that has both short-run and long-run human consequences for those involved as well as repercussions for others. Moreover, the workers in PE have specific information permitting them to consider the well-being of other workers and consumers. And PE's participatory workers know they are consumers and that their consumption depends on total production, which in turn depends on their work proposals. But while these features of production in PE are not included in FMPE, we do model workers' councils in FMPE as centers of human activity that affect the immediate well-being and future characteristics of those participating as well as the prospects of others in the economy.

Constraints

In PE, actors know that job complexes will be balanced across workplaces and that consumption is tied to work effort. This makes it advisable for workers to make proposals that maximize overall social welfare since under equitable arrangements this also maximizes the benefits to each. But in FMPE we do not assume workers necessarily understand this. Instead, we assume workers in each council, WC(j), make proposals to maximize their own well-being and development from work, $W(j) = W(U(j), \Delta C(j))$. But in attempting to maximize their own well being workers' councils will be subject to some constraints. For example:

1. We do not want some workers working short hours, or at a leisurely pace, or in luxury conditions while others work long hours, or at breakneck speed, or in dangerous conditions.

2. We do not want some workers' experiences to be significantly more "empowering" than others.

3. We do not want some workplaces using excessive quantities of scarce resources, valuable machinery, and produced inputs to generate very little or unwanted output.

4. We do not want people trained as mining engineers working in road construction while civil engineers work in mines.

Constraints 3 and 4 are typical of the traditional economic demand for productive efficiency and are explicitly addressed in our formal model, but we choose not to address constraints 1 and 2 this way. We want workers to make their own work lives as fulfilling and empowering as possible without presuming a more privileged position for themselves. We could require the planning procedure to equalize work conditions in all councils, so that in addition to each worker within a council having a situation comparable to that of all others in the same council, each council would have the same average conditions as every other. We reject this approach because it destroys diversity, is unnecessarily inefficient, and tends to reduce the quality of worklife to the lowest common denominator. Instead we allow councils to develop very different work conditions from one another but require that workers in councils with nonaverage work conditions balance their work time among two or more councils so all workers enjoy comparable effects.

In other words, in FMPE we assume that different groups of workers participate in the planning process by attempting to maximize the quality of work life in their primary workers' council subject only to constraints that address points 3 and 4. After the plan is settled workers split time between units so as to address points 1 and 2. So the planning procedure in FMPE is responsible for addressing inefficiencies (3 and 4), while inequities and disparate empowerment (1 and 2) are addressed in a post-planning shuffling of assignments and schedules organized by economywide Job Complex Committees.

Therefore, in FMPE we treat workers' councils in a way analogous to the way we treated consumers' councils. Each workers' council tries to maximize the total well-being of its members' work experience subject to the constraint that it be as useful to the rest of society in any work that it performs as any other *equally endowed* workers' council.

Different Productive Endowments

Specifying "equally endowed" is key to modeling production in FMPE. A particular workers' council is defined by its members' training and skills and by the physical productive assets (plant and equipment) at its disposal. That is, all workers' councils have unique productive capabilities, but not all workers' councils are created equal. Some have greater per capita capabilities, some less. We do not want some well-endowed workers' councils taking advantage of other less well-endowed ones by making proposals that for lesser endowed councils would represent considerable work efforts and sacrifices, but for a council with a large endowment represents insufficient efforts.

But how do we define and measure "equally endowed"? And even if there is an effective way to classify workers' councils (WCs) into different groups that are "equally endowed" with respect to productive capabilities, how can we measure the extent to which one group of "equally endowed" WCs is more or less capable than another? Ultimately all WCs' proposals must be measured against one another in order for participants in the planning procedure to judge which proposals represent acceptable efforts and merit approval, and which do not.

—84—

As with consumption, indicative prices play a critical role comparing the productive endowments of different WCs. If, as in the case of consumers' councils (CCs), we assume a vector of known indicative prices, we can measure productive capabilities of any WC as well as the social costs of any intermediate inputs it requests and the social usefulness of the outputs it proposes to deliver.

In thinking about how to define FMPE, it is clear that a "circulating capital" model is inappropriate since this approach would fail to clarify what distinguishes one WC from another. In a circulating capital approach, differential productive endowments disappear as no unit is characterized by anything other than an identifying number. Likewise, in a Debreuvian model the different production units are distinguished by different production possibility sets, but not because the firms in the models each begin with particular machinery or with personnel having particular skills and knowledge. In Debreuvian models each production center has a unique book of productive blueprints—hence the differential profits that accrue to different firms in Debreuvian competitive solutions. But certainly the first thing a participatory economy would do is publish all its books of blueprints! It follows that we cannot usefully employ Debreuvian assumptions. In Sraffian or Von Neuman models industries are defined but all firms in an industry are presumed to have access to the same technology, and to use the same technology to produce their product(s). Clearly this will not help us represent WCs as units with distinct human/physical productive capabilities.

In sum, we want to recognize the existence of particular people with particular historical work experiences, skills, and capabilities. We cannot quantify all aspects of what makes workers' councils unique. For example, the social relations established by having worked together in the past cannot be captured in FMPE. But we can account for scarce skills and training and for productive characteristics of plant and equipment of particular vintages.

Workers' Councils

What will make WCs distinct is the combination of human and physical assets they begin with. These consist of the productive characteristics of the members of the WC, and the plant and machines the WC has when planning begins. With this in mind, we are ready to define the production side of FMPE.

Let l_j be the vector of the number of units of each category of labor present in the initial membership of WC(j), where

$$\sum_j l_j = l*$$

Let k_j be the vector of initial capital stocks (plant and equipment) that characterize WC(j) where

$$\sum_j k_j = k*$$

And let $\hat{k}_j$ be the vector of the number of units of each category of capital good WC(j) proposes to add to or release from its initial capital stock, and $\hat{l}_j$ be the vector of the number of units of each category of labor WC(j) proposes to add or release. Then, each WC(j) will initially be "charged" for its productive resources an amount

$$p_k k_j + p_l l_j$$

which defines the extent to which socially useful outputs can be reasonably expected.

If the WC(j) is willing to be charged for more productive labor or wishes to be charged for less, it can submit as part of its proposal at any iteration $\hat{l}_{ij} > 0$ (demanding more of the ith labor type) or $\hat{l}_{ij} < 0$ (releasing some of the ith labor type). Similarly, if the WC(j) wants to request more or release some of its previous capital stock, it can submit as part of its proposal at any iteration $\hat{k}_{ij} > 0$ (demanding more of capital type i), or $\hat{k}_{ij} < 0$ (releasing some of capital type i). Note that the assumption that no new capital or labor types become available to the economy as a whole in the period means that

$$\sum_j \hat{l}_{ij} = 0 \text{ and } \sum_j \hat{k}_{ij} = 0 \quad \text{for all i}$$

So, if we let $\hat{a}_j$ be WC(j)'s vector of proposed inputs of produced goods and $\hat{r}_j$ be WC(j)'s vector of proposed inputs of resources, it follows that

$$p_a \hat{a}_j + p_k(k_j + \hat{k}_j) + p_l(l_j + \hat{l}_j) + p_r \hat{r}_j$$

represents the social value of the inputs WC(j) is requesting in its proposal, plus the social value of its productive endowment, corrected for proposed additions and releases. If $\hat{y}_j$ is the vector of outputs WC(j) proposes to supply, then $p\hat{y}_j$ is the social value of those outputs, and as long as

$$p_a \hat{a}_j + p_k (k_j + \hat{k}_j) + p_l (l_j + \hat{l}_j) + p_r \hat{r}_j \leq p\hat{y}_j$$

WC(j)'s proposal will not be what we might call "socially abusive." (Recall that the dual of the societal programming problem finds shadow prices such that

$$p_k K + p_l L + p_r R \geq v (I - A)$$

with strict equality for any activity that forms part of the optimal solution.)

In formal models of traditional economies, production units are assumed to maximize

$$p\hat{y}_j - \left\{ p_a\hat{a}_j + p_k(k_j + \hat{k}_j) + p_l(l_j + \hat{l}_j) + p_r\hat{r}_j \right\}$$

subject to the constraint of known technology. In our model, however, WCs try to maximize their member's well-being—that is, their fulfillment and development—subject to the above constraint. We let U(j) represent the members' immediate fulfillment and ΔC(j) represent their development so that W(j) = W(U(j),ΔC(j)) represents their well-being function.

Differences from Participatory Production

Once again, our model approximates but does not fully represent participatory production.

1. There is a difference in what workers take into account in making their choices. In FMPE, producers try to maximize their own well-being assuming that it does not depend on others.

Again, constraints ensure that equity is not violated, but no empathy is assumed, and no solidarity enhancing features are incorporated.

2. FMPE includes no mechanism for the use of qualitative data.

Again, as we will see, this difference proves not to diminish the likelihood that PE will perform as well as FMPE.

3. No federations of workers' councils are explicitly defined in FMPE.

Again, we will discover that by interpreting some WC(j)s as geographcially based federations and some as industry federations, production externalities and economies of scale can be accounted for in FMPE in ways that reflect how they would be treated in PE.

Formal Summary of Councils' Goals

At this point we can summarize the problems facing consumers' and workers' councils in FMPE. The problem for a typical consumer council, CC(h), is

$$\text{maximize } W(h) = W\ (U(h), \Delta C(h)) \ \text{ s.t.}$$

$$\left\{ p_k K + p_l L + p_r R \right\} (I - A)^{-1} \left[\hat{y}_h - \hat{y}_a \right] \leq 0$$

where $\hat{y}_a$ is the average consumption bundle requested so that this expression represents an equitable budget constraint on consumers in FMPE.

The problem facing a typical workers' council, WC(j), is:

$$\text{maximize } W(j) = W(U(j), \Delta C(j))$$

$$\text{s.t. } \ p_k(k_j + \hat{k}_j) + p_l(l_j + \hat{l}_j) + p_a\hat{a}_j + p_r\hat{r}_j \leq p_y\hat{y}_j$$

which says workers are free to maximize the quality of work life as long as the social value of their contribution to output exceeds the social costs they incurred in producing it.

Now if the well-being functions of consumers' councils had all the convexity properties traditionally assumed in formal analyses for individual consumer's exogenous preferences, the consumption constraint above, read as an equality, would be a separating hyperplane between CC(h)'s "at least as preferred consumption set" and the "socially nonabusive" (not too greedy) consumption set. And if the well-being functions of workers' councils had similar convexity properties and workers' council's production possibility sets had the same convexity properties usually assumed, then the production constraint above, read as an equality, would be a separating hyperplane between WC(j)'s "at least as preferred production set" and its "socially nonabusive" (not too lazy) production set. Under these assumptions, objectives of CCs and WCs could be integrated by the planning procedure presented below to yield familiar convergence and optimality properties. That is, the formal participatory model, FMPE, whose nonmarket, noncentrally planned procedures we describe formally below, proves at least as viable and desirable as familiar market and central planning models.

It is worth noting the similarity between the planning problems faced by CCs and WCs in FMPE. This formal equivalence reflects our underlying insight that work and consumption are each instances of social economic activity that always affect the well-being of those immediately involved as well as the prospects of others. So, in the case of both consumption and production, the choice problem, as we conceive it, is for groups of people to pursue their own well-being subject to the constraint of social responsibility, which in our view translates into granting others equal means to achieve their goals as they see them.

Allocation

We now add a Planning Bureau, PB, that accumulates no information and recalls no information from previous iterations. As a matter of fact, since the PB's functions in FMPE can be described as a mechanical algorithm, all its functions could be automated. And we are ready to give a formal description of FMPE's decentralized planning procedure.

The actors in the social, iterative, planning process are consumers' councils CC(h)s, workers' councils, WC(j)s, and the planning bureau, PB. In total, FMPE is a variant of a well-known price-guided procedure originally developed by Oscar Lange, Kenneth Arrow, and Leonid Hurwicz.

1. Each CC(h) makes an arbitrary, initial proposal, $\hat{y}_h$.

Since FMPE consumption proposals may be arbitrary, realistic PE consumption proposals made in light of last year's plan, indicative prices, and expected or desired growth should require fewer iterations to converge.

2. Each WC(j) makes an arbitrary initial proposal, $\{\hat{y}_j, \hat{a}_j, \hat{k}_j, \hat{l}_j, \hat{r}_j\}$, also reporting its initial endowment, $\{k_j, l_j\}$.

Again, the fact that FMPE allows the initial proposal to be arbitrary means PE proposals based on last year's indicative prices and workers' knowledge of consumer and worker desires expressed in early iterations last year should converge in fewer iterations.

3. The PB quotes an arbitrary price vector $\hat{P} = [\hat{p}, \hat{p}_k, \hat{p}_l, \hat{p}_r]$.

Usually this is taken to be $\hat{P} = (1...1...1)$. In PE we have suggested that facilitation board employees would calculate anticipated prices based on the prior year's final prices adjusted for likely changes. Whether this calculation is according to a formula or left to the skills of iteration workers, it cannot diminish PE's capacity to attain desirable ends attained by FMPE, and should reduce the number of necessary iterations.

4. Each CC(h) changes its request for good i according to the rule:

$$\Delta y_{ih} = 0 \text{ if } \hat{y}_{ih} = 0 \text{ and } \left\{ \frac{\delta W(h)}{\delta y_{ih}} - q_h p_i \right\} < 0$$

$$\Delta y_{ih} = \alpha \left\{ \frac{\delta W(h)}{\delta y_{ih}} - q_h p_i \right\} \text{ otherwise}$$

$$\text{where } q_h = \frac{\delta W(h)}{\delta I(a)} \text{ and}$$

$$I(a) = \frac{p \hat{y}_N}{H} \text{ and}$$

$\hat{y}_N$ = the total net production vector proposed by all WC in step 2:

$$\hat{y}_N = \sum_j (\hat{y}_j - \hat{a}_j) \text{ and}$$

H = number of consumers councils

and α = an adjustment coefficient between 0 and 1: $0 < \alpha < 1$

This merely says:

a. If a CC estimates that the increase in its well-being from obtaining a first unit of good i is less than the value of what it will be "charged" by other councils for the resources producing good i requires, it should not ask for any good i.

b. If a CC estimates that the change in its well-being from obtaining an additional unit of good i is greater (less) than the value of what it will be "charged" by other councils for the resources producing good i requires, the CC should increase (decrease) its request for good i by some fraction of the discrepancy.

It should be clear that this implies that consumers' councils will change their requests whenever the difference between social benefits and social costs would be increased by doing so. If CCs in FMPE propose no changes it is because they have reached local optima, having satisfied the necessary and sufficient Kuhn-Tucker conditions. The difference in PE is only that estimates of social cost are based not only on current indicative prices—which is the only thing considered in the formal model—but qualitative information including graphic descriptions of the human consequences of producing and consuming different goods. Again, the additional information available in PE can only improve the quality of estimates of true social costs and benefits. It is also the case that adjustments in PE are not confined to an arbitrary proportionality factor that is independent of the degree of excess demand and supply.

5. Each WC changes its proposal by increasing, decreasing, or leaving unchanged the $\hat{a}_{ij}$, $\hat{k}_{ij}$, $\hat{r}_{ij}$, $\hat{l}_{ij}$, and implicitly $\hat{y}_{ij}$ according to the following rules.

$$\Delta a_{ij} = 0 \text{ if } \hat{a}_{ij} = 0 \text{ and } \left\{ \frac{\delta W(j)}{\delta(a_{ij})} + p \frac{\delta y(j)}{\delta a(ij)} - p_i \right\} < 0$$

$$\Delta a_{ij} = \beta \left\{ \frac{\delta W(j)}{\delta(a_{ij})} + p \frac{\delta y(j)}{\delta a(ij)} - p_i \right\} \text{ otherwise}$$

$$\Delta k_{ij} = 0 \text{ if } \left(k_{ij} + \hat{k}_{ij} \right) = 0 \text{ and } \left\{ \frac{\delta W(j)}{\delta(k_{ij})} + p \frac{\delta y(j)}{\delta k(ij)} - p_{ki} \right\} < 0$$

$$\Delta k_{ij} = \beta \left\{ \frac{\delta W(j)}{\delta(k_{ij})} + p \frac{\delta y(j)}{\delta k(ij)} - p_{ki} \right\} \text{ otherwise}$$

$$\Delta l_{ij} = 0 \text{ if } \left(l_{ij} + \hat{l}_{ij} \right) = 0 \text{ and } \left\{ \frac{\delta W(j)}{\delta(l_{ij})} + p \frac{\delta y(j)}{\delta l(ij)} - p_{li} \right\} < 0$$

$$\Delta l_{ij} = \beta \left\{ \frac{\delta W(j)}{\delta(l_{ij})} + p \frac{\delta y(j)}{\delta l(ij)} - p_{li} \right\} \text{ otherwise}$$

$$\Delta r_{ij} = 0 \text{ if } \hat{r}_{ij} = 0 \text{ and } \left\{ \frac{\delta W(j)}{\delta(r_{ij})} + p \frac{\delta y(j)}{\delta r(ij)} - p_{ri} \right\} < 0$$

$$\Delta r_{ij} = \beta \left\{ \frac{\delta W(j)}{\delta(r_{ij})} + p \frac{\delta y(j)}{\delta r(ij)} - p_{ri} \right\} \text{ otherwise}$$

where β = an adjustment coefficient between zero and 1: $0 < \beta < 1$

Remember that other councils primarily judge workers' councils' proposals with an eye to the relation between the social benefits of their outputs and the social costs of their inputs. These rules together express the idea that if changing the input/output mix increases net social benefits a workers' council will implement the change. Or if the increased well-being of the workers involved outweighs any excess of social cost over social benefits to others that accompany the change, the change will be enacted. But this implies that whenever producers can adjust production to generate a positive net social benefit, they will. The fact that PE provides additional qualitative information beyond indicative prices means PE's actors will better estimate social costs and benefits. Likewise, more flexible adjustment coefficients can facilitate more rapid convergence. Moreover, PE employs various rules limiting responses of actors during some iterations. The advantage is that these devices can accelerate convergence. The disadvantage is that they may induce minor inequalities and inefficiencies. The trick, of course, is to choose regulations whose time savings are more valuable than inequalities or inefficiencies introduced.

6. The PB changes prices $\hat{P} = [\hat{p}, \hat{p}_k, \hat{p}_l, \hat{p}_r]$ according to the following rules

$$\Delta p_i = 0 \text{ if } \hat{p}_i = 0 \text{ and } \left\{ \sum_h \hat{y}_{hi} + \sum_j \left(\hat{a}_{ij} - \hat{y}_{ij} \right) \right\} < 0$$

$$\Delta p_i = \gamma \left\{ \sum_h \hat{y}_{hi} + \sum_j \left(\hat{a}_{ij} - \hat{y}_{ij} \right) \right\} \text{ otherwise}$$

$$\Delta p_{ki} = 0 \text{ if } \hat{p}_{ki} = 0 \text{ and } \sum_j \hat{k}_{ij} < 0$$

$$\Delta p_{ki} = \gamma \sum_j \hat{k}_{ij} \text{ otherwise}$$

$$\Delta p_{li} = 0 \text{ if } \hat{p}_{li} = 0 \text{ and } \sum_j \hat{l}_{ij} < 0$$

$$\Delta p_{li} = \gamma \sum_j \hat{l}_{ij} \text{ otherwise}$$

$$\Delta p_{ri} = 0 \text{ if } \hat{p}_{ri} = 0 \text{ and } \left\{ \sum_j \hat{r}_{ij} - r*_i \right\} < 0$$

$$\Delta p_{ri} = \gamma \left\{ \sum_j \hat{r}_{ij} - r*_i \right\} \text{ otherwise}$$

where $\gamma =$ an adjustment coefficient between zero and 1: $0 < \gamma < 1$

These rules raise prices for goods in excess demand and lower prices for goods in excess supply, thereby moving proposals toward a feasible plan. The difference between PE and FMPE here is that in FMPE price adjustments are always the same arbitrary percentage of excess demands, whereas PE adjustments can vary to hasten convergence. We leave discussion of this to chapter 6.

The rest of the planning procedure in FMPE simply repeats steps 1 to 6 until there are no further changes. The proof that this procedure, which, as we indicated, is a variant of a procedure developed by

Lange, Arrow, and Hurwicz,[1] will converge to a feasible and optimal plan under the usual convexity assumptions can be found in chapter 4 of *The Theory of Economic Planning* by G.M. Heal (Amsterdam: North Holland Press, 1973).[2]

While it is mathematically equivalent, economically, our procedure differs substantially from the Lange-Arrow-Hurwicz procedure discussed by Heal. We have consumers' councils maximizing their well-being subject to constraint while Heal stipulates an overall social welfare function. And we have workers' councils maximizing their well-being subject to a constraint, whereas Heal stipulates profit maximization. However, these economic differences notwithstanding, the convergence proof Heal outlines for the Lange-Arrow-Hurwicz procedure applies to our procedure as well.

What our social iterative procedure essentially does is "whittle down" infeasible proposals from both consumers' and workers' councils in two different ways.

1. Unjustifiable consumer "greediness" is reduced by the refusal of other consumers' councils to approve requests that require a greater than per capita use of society's scarce productive resources while unjustifiable worker "laziness" is reduced by refusal of other workers' councils to approve requests that entail less than average work effort. This kind of whittling is expressed in the constraint inequalities for consumers' and workers' councils dictated by equity.

2. At the same time, excess demand for particularly scarce inputs and socially costly outputs are whittled down by raising

---

1. K. Arrow, L. Hurwicz, and H. Uzawa, *Studies in Linear and Nonlinear Programming* (Stanford: Stanford University Press, 1958).
2. The proof hinges on stability properties of gradient procedures for finding saddle points which are in J. LaSalle and S. Lefschetz, "Stability in Liapunov's direct method, with applications," *Volume 4: Mathematics in Science and Engineering* (New York: Academic Press, 1961). An extension of the stability theorem to cover discontinuities in the rate of change of variables when boundaries are reached and when non-negativity constraints become binding can be found in C. Henry, "Differential equations with dicontinuous right-hand sides in mathematical economics," *Journal of Economic Theory 4*, no. 3 (1972).

the indicative prices that units requesting them are "charged" while excess supplies of plentiful outputs and socially inexpensive inputs are reduced by lowering the indicative prices that units requesting them are charged. Wherever possible, these changes in relative prices induce optimizing councils to "shift" their requests rather than "reduce" their requests, so that equity and efficiency are generated simultaneously.

In technical terms, convergence and optimality hinge on the convexity properties of our consumers' and workers' councils' well-being functions and the production possibility sets of producers. But while convexity of production possibility sets is a well known issue, the convexity properties of our council well-being functions are not. Moreover, our consumers' councils differ from the consumers of traditional theory in three important ways. First, our consumers' councils consist of a number of people whose individual preferences presumably differ. Second, some consumers' councils in FMPE are lower level neighborhood councils, but others are higher level federations of councils so that the well-being functions of some councils are really the well-being functions of groups of neighborhoods, wards, or states for public goods. And third, while we could have treated preferences as exogenous in FMPE and recognized only "preference fulfillment effects" of consumption choices, we insisted on allowing for endogenous preferences and recognizing the importance of "preference development effects" as well. We reviewed our reasons for doing this in chapter 1 and developed a rigorous analysis in chapter 6 of *Welfare Economics* where we also explained why, in our view, the more realistic assumption of endogenous preferences makes traditional assumptions of convexity less plausible.

Our modeling of workers' councils is even further removed from traditional treatments of production. Besides treating group rather than individual preferences for work life and recognizing the preference development as well as preference fulfillment effects of work choices, we have formulated worker choice in the same terms as consumer choice. Since this is unusual, there has been very little previous discussion of what the convexity properties of such preference orderings might be like.

However, in our opinion, for most economists convexity assumptions have long been an assumption of convenience rather than conviction. The reasons for doubting the plausibility of convexity assumptions necessary for proving the existence of equilibria in market economies and convergence to feasible plans in different versions of central planning are compelling and well known. And of course recognizing the endogeneity of preferences adds yet another reason for doubting that reality is conveniently convex. But historically the necessity of ignoring these doubts in order to proceed with formal analyses has been, for the economists concerned, more compelling still. In this vein, we do not see that working through the logic of our economic model under what are admittedly dubious convexity assumptions is any different than doing the same for traditional models of more familiar economic systems. It is a reasonable procedure in treating formal models precisely insofar as it illustrates one important respect in which real systems, like PE, *should* diverge from formal models, like FMPE, if they are to prove useful. Some of the differences between allocation procedures in PE and FMPE are necessary, that is, because the convexity assumptions required to guarantee convergence for FMPE cannot be expected to hold in the real world setting of PE.

Summary

We have presented a "well-defined" formal model of an economic system quite different from familiar formal models of individualistic consumption and hierarchical production integrated by markets or central planning. FMPE has participatory, social, and equitable properties consistent with our version of PE and we have demonstrated how under the same assumptions necessary to prove coherence and optimality in familiar models, FMPE will also converge to a feasible, Pareto optimal plan. This provides an answer to Allen Buchanan's request for a "well-developed theoretical model of the nonmarket system."

As we explained in chapter 3, if higher level federations of consumers' councils participate in the planning process equally with neighborhood councils—proposing and revising requests for "public goods" appropriate to their level—and if individuals are "charged" their proportionate share of the social costs of those requests, there is no incentive to misrepresent preferences for public goods or to try to "ride for free." Moreover, federations provide realistic settings for implementing further refinements consistent with efficiency along the lines of demand revealing and pivot mechanisms discussed in the theoretical public finance literature. In sum, if we recognize that some CC(h)s in FMPE are higher level federations and assume a gradation of federations that corresponds to gradations in differences between issues of local and central finance, FMPE generates accurate estimates of social benefits for public as well as private goods, and correspondingly optimal plans.

The geographic-based federations of workers' councils permit analogous consideration of production externalities. In the traditional example of downstream producers, the federation of workers' councils along the stream would express the "demand" for clean water for production purposes. There is neither incentive for the federation to exaggerate the benefit of clean water to them—since there is no issue of "compensation" for damages—nor is there incentive to underestimate the negative impact of a pollutant. The polluter may have a short-run incentive to underreport the amount of pollution since the workers' council responsible will be "charged" a negative indicative price times the quantity of pollution released, but this incentive is no different from an incentive to underreport the stock of machinery on hand or skill levels of members, since workers' councils are also held responsible for these productive assets. In both cases, accurate measurements of "inputs" and "outputs" are necessary, but this is true in any economy. The advantage of FMPE is its ability to generate accurate evaluations of external effects assuming that the physical quantities can be reasonably estimated.

About half a century ago, Oscar Lange, Abba Lerner, and Frederick Taylor, responded to an erroneous consensus that public enterprise economies could not operate efficiently by elaborating a model of what they called a "socialist" economy that they argued was capable of yielding Pareto optimal outcomes. While not an end to the "socialist calculation debate," their model served as a powerful challenge to what had become a firmly held "impossibility" conviction among economists regarding the supposed inability of public enterprise systems to yield efficient results. Interestingly, their formal model was derived directly from propositions well known to microeconomists of their day.[1]

Our formal model of a participatory economy also relies heavily on work well known to microeconomic theorists. The planning procedure is a variation of a "price guided" procedure well known to those familiar with the literature on iterative planning mechanisms that flourished briefly in the late 1960s and early 1970s. It is true that this literature focused on solving what was considered at that time the principal problem of central planning—how the central planning bureau could gather information about the technical capabilities of different units—while our focus is to adapt iterative procedures so that the different units in the economy can participate directly in forging an equitable, efficient plan *without* the intervention of any central planning bureau. But as in the case of Lange, Lerner, and Taylor, the techniques we use have been familiar to microeconomic theorists for decades. We hope our formal model will also challenge unwarranted pessimism among economists, namely that there is no alternative allocation mechanism to markets or central planning. Decentralized planning in which groups of workers and consumers participate directly in arranging their own economic endeavors is not only feasible, it is highly desirable.

Formal Models Versus Reality

In our view, economic theorists have often engaged in a kind of deception we do not wish to continue. Based on a legitimate appeal to the practical necessity of abstracting from countless intricacies in order to focus on a relatively few key relations for the purpose of discovering their non-intuitive consequences, economists have constructed abstract, formal models of different economic systems. The most familiar is the "ideal" model of a competitive, private enter-

---

1. For an accessible modern rendition of their work see Oscar Lange and Frederick Taylor, *On the Economic Theory of Socialism* (New York: Monthly Review Press, 1964).

prise, market economy known to all who have taken a course in microeconomic theory as "perfectly competitive capitalism." But similar "ideal" models of centrally planned public enterprise economies and variants of public enterprise market economies have been constructed as well. The deception arises not in the derivations of conclusions from stipulated assumptions, but in the examination of the realism of the assumptions and the consequent need to question the realism of the conclusions derived from those assumptions. In particular, conclusions about the desirability of different economic institutions and systems as well as policy recommendations that stem from conclusions drawn from formal models without attempting to estimate the effects of predictable discrepancies between reality and the model's assumptions can be very deceptive. Here we summarize the most important differences between the assumptions of FMPE and the reality of PE, and between the procedures of FMPE and the procedures of PE in order to assess the plausibility and usefulness of the conclusions derived from FMPE for our assessment of PE itself. But first we summarize our assessment of traditional alternatives in the same light.

Ideal Markets Versus Reality

If real markets equilibrate instantaneously, *if* real market structures are competitive, *if* real buyers and sellers have perfect knowledge of all prices (past and future), and *if* there are really no externalities or public goods, *then and only then* would formal models allow us to conclude that real market systems will yield prices that accurately reflect true social benefits and costs and Pareto optimal allocations of resources and goods. But if any of these assumptions are not met in real systems, real market prices will mis-specify real social costs and benefits and real market allocations will be socially inefficient. It is not our purpose to review the vast literature on market disequilibria, market imperfections, and market failures. All these are important, but in our opinion the pervasiveness of external effects is alone sufficient to render market failure ubiquitous, and consequently, to render market misallocation the rule, not the exception, as we have explained at length in *Welfare Economics*. But the point is this: (1) To the extent the assumptions of formal models are unwarranted, the model's conclusions about efficient allocations of resources are unwarranted as well. (2) There are ample reasons to doubt the plausibility of some if not all the assumptions for market models. Our two contributions to the skeptical literature on markets have been to argue that external effects are pervasive, and that the bias against providing goods with greater than average positive external effects inherent in any conceivable real world market economy, in context of endogenous preferences, will lead to ever increasing inefficiencies.[1]

One approach for dealing with public goods is the Groves-Ledyard demand-revealing mechanism in which individuals report to the government their marginal willingness to pay for all quantities of every public good. I report how much I am willing to pay for one missile, two missiles,...one road, two roads,...and so on. The government supplies a level of each public good such that the marginal social cost of production equals the sum of the marginal willingness to pay of all consumers. Each individual is then taxed according to her or his proportionate share of the total expenditure minus the reported consumer surplus of all others. I pay my share of the cost of all public goods minus the difference between what all other citizens have said they would be willing to pay for the amounts provided and their proportionate share, and so does everyone else. The critical idea is that my tax bill is effectively independent of what I myself report to the government regarding my taste for public goods. I cannot lower my bill by reporting inaccurate information. The only thing I can do by giving information to the government is influence the amount of each public good provided, and I can do this best by accurately reporting my preferences for public goods.

Theoretically, it works. But note that each individual has to report to the government her or his desires for every possible quantity of every public good. It is not simply that we have to say how much we think should be delivered. We must say how much we would like the delivery of each possible amount of every public good. Imagine the information apparatus necessary to communicate all this. It is an information flow comparable with what participatory economies require for the entire economy because, while dealing with fewer

---

1. See chapter 7 in *Welfare Economics*.

goods, it addresses a much broader scope of quantities. Now imagine incorporating this entire apparatus on top of a market system. The "public goods sector" would approach an information capability sufficient to allow collective self-management along the lines of PE, but the "superior" system would be used for only a subsector of the economy. Trying to introduce the Groves-Ledyard corrective mechanism would ultimately subvert the market system.

Ideal Central Planning Versus Reality

A similar argument applies to central planning. *If* real central planners knew the technical capabilities of all production units (or *if* there were incentive compatible procedures to induce real units to reveal their true capabilities to central authorities), *if* real planners knew all primary resources availabilities, *if* real planners knew the relative social benefits of all goods, *if* real planners could count on their orders being faithfully executed, *if* real jobs were assigned and goods distributed efficiently, and *if* nobody valued having decision making input in proportion to the degree they were affected by the outcome, *then and only then* would formal models of centrally planned economies allow us to predict Pareto optimal outcomes for real centrally planned economies. While we find usual "Western" assessments of the information and incentive problems of central planning more skeptical than warranted—particularly in light of an asymmetrical unwillingness to examine the assumptions behind market models with a similarly critical eye—we nonetheless concur that discrepancies between realistic central planning and formal models of central planning make it naive to translate conclusions from the formal models to the real world.

In realistic systems, where a coordinator class substitutes its own welfare function for that of ordinary citizens, obviously central planning does not maximize social welfare. Yet, even if this could be avoided, there is no way to eliminate the bias against self-managed work opportunities inherent in even the most democratic central planning without eliminating the basic hierarchical decision making relation defining central planning. But once we entertain the idea of doing this, we would have to institute new means of information dissemination that would move us toward participatory economics. On the other hand, if we maintain central planning's inherent bias against self-management, then central planning would inevitably involve a spiral of authoritarianism/passivity and associated snowballing divergence from Pareto optimality, as proved in *Welfare Economics*.

FMPE Versus PE

Besides "practical" problems of disequilibria and market imperfections, the principal discrepancy between formal models of market economies and real world market systems is the pervasiveness of external effects in the latter. Besides "practical" information and incentive problems, the principal discrepancy between formal models of centrally planned economies and real centrally planned economies is that it does matter to real people who decides what they will do. Not surprisingly, the price of ignoring these discrepancies is failure to understand the fundamental deficiencies as well as practical problems of market and centrally planned allocations. That is, accepting conclusions from formal models that fail to recognize that human beings are distinguished by their ability and desire to make choices about how to conduct their lives (models of central planning), and formal models that fail to recognize that human beings are a social species, and therefore that our economic activities are characterized by varying degrees of external effects (models of market economies), risks seriously misestimating the usefulness of these allocative mechanisms to real human beings.

The question now is whether conclusions derived from FMPE could be deceiving as well. First, FMPE was specifically designed with what we believe are the fundamental inadequacies of markets and central planning in mind. By including "nested" federations of consumers' and workers' councils among our actors in the planning system, we have accounted for complex sociality in human economic endeavors at the ground level of our economy rather than pretending sociality is a rare and unimportant occurrence or compensating for it as an afterthought. And by having workers' and consumers' councils propose and revise their own activities we have guaranteed "grass-roots" participation. But this is not to say that FMPE is completely sensitive to human sociality and self-management.

FMPE includes federations of councils only via the theoretical artifice of interpreting CC(h)s conveniently. While such artifices—like the Debruvian artifice of treating time by interpreting the same good in different time periods as different goods—are useful, they are also often unsatisfactory in important respects. In our case there is a lot more to the integration of federations into the real planning process in PE than is indicated by the formal treatment in FMPE. FMPE also operates entirely at the level of workers' and consumers' collectives, which leaves individual participation out of the formal model. However, PE includes individual worker proposals and permits living units and their members to propose their own individual consumption activities.

More significantly, in FMPE actors have no qualitative information concerning one another and are not assumed to behave out of empathetic feelings. The flow of qualitative information we described in PE is deleted in FMPE simply because it is difficult to formalize. On the other hand, we assume actors in FMPE are motivated by individual self-interest and never by empathy for an important reason. The reason is *not* that we believe human beings are incapable of acting out of concern for others, since we believe they do so under propitious circumstances and frequently even in situations that discourage such behavior. Nor is the reason that we attach little importance to solidarity in evaluating economic affairs. Quite the contrary, we consider promoting solidarity one of the chief virtues an economic system can claim. Instead, we assume actors in FMPE operate entirely out of self-interest in order to answer legitimate objections from skeptics.

That is, if the kind of economy we espouse could only function efficiently if actors made choices based on concern for one another, it would only be of value for people who have already achieved a high degree of mutual concern. But we claim to have designed an economy that *promotes* solidarity by overcoming mistrust and antagonisms based on real historical experiences of exploitation and oppression by building a legacy of equitable, mutually beneficial institutions. That is, we claim individual self-interest coincides with the social interest in PE, and PE's institutions lead people to take the interests of others as seriously as they take their own when making decisions.

So, we reiterate, the conclusions of FMPE are not based on any assumption of empathetic behavior on actors' parts. In FMPE actors are assumed to be the same "homo-economi" as in traditional models—doing the best they can for themselves under the circumstances in which they find themselves. In PE there is additional qualitative information provided that promotes development of solidarity and in PE there are opportunities for granting exceptions to rules concerning effort and consumption based on empathy for others' needs. Thus, to the extent that real human behavior in PE deviates from individual self-interest and incorporates a degree of solidarity, PE will function *better* than conclusions from FMPE predict.

In sum, while no real economy will ever achieve perfect estimates of social costs and benefits of all production and consumption choices, and consequently no real economy will ever reach a Pareto optimum, we do not believe PE would be characterized by the *systematic* biases inherent in traditional economic systems. Participatory economies would not be biased against activities with greater than average positive "external" effects and would not make it more difficult for people to engage in self-managed work than necessitated by real technological and resource constraints. Still, if imperfections are inevitable, and if endogenous preferences inevitably magnify initial imperfections over time as we have argued in *Welfare Economics,* will not PE eventually careen down some increasingly nonoptimal trajectory, even if it is a different one than those traveled by centrally planned and market economies?

To the extent that people are capable of "purposeful preference molding" or "informed self-development," biases in economies *will* become magnified over time and systematic nonoptimalities *will* snowball, as we spelled out in *Welfare Economics*. But this does not imply that pursuit of economic efficiency is hopeless. The key is that *systematic* biases will lead to snowballing divergences from optimal allocations. However, if biases are random in the sense that a kind of activity that is "overpriced" one period is just as likely to be "underpriced" as "overpriced" the next, there is no way individuals can adjust to benefit and thereby produce the socially counterproductive effect of aggravating the bias further. So if FMPE contains no *systematic* biases, then inevitable misestimations in PE need not

—104—

yield a spiral of increasing divergence from optimality. Moreover, the generation of developmental effects of economic choices that would be the basis of many exceptions to formal rules in FMPE granted in PE would provide an environment sensitive to detecting and correcting deleterious effects of endogenous preference development.

Conclusion

In the context of pervasive externalities and desires for self-management we have shown that: (1) realistic market and centrally planned economies will do far worse than their unrealistic formal models. Far from achieving optimality, once crucial unrealistic assumptions are recognized as assumptions of convenience, each of these familiar systems are seen to contain a systematic bias. Moreover, we have explained why in the context of endogenous preferences systematic biases inevitably lead to a snowballing divergence from Pareto optimal allocations and therefore to increasing degradation of human possibilities. We have also explained why we believe correctives require interactions that would be impossible and/or unstable in these flawed institutional contexts. On the other hand, we have shown that (2) a formal model of a participatory economy, FMPE, in which actors are assumed to behave only in accord with individual self-interest, will achieve Pareto optimality even in the context of external effects and desires for self-management. Moreover, we have argued that realistic versions of participatory economies, PE, should do still better than FMPE. That is, divergences between formal models and real world versions of participatory economies are likely to be self-correcting, whereas just the opposite is the case for formal models and real world versions of market and centrally planned economies. In sum:

1. In the traditional world of abstract formal models, participatory economies deserve to be considered an equally viable alternative to perfectly competitive capitalist and coordinator market and centrally planned economies.

2. Formal models of participatory economies achieve Pareto optimality under far less restrictive and more realistic assumptions than formal models of market and centrally planned economies.

3. Realistic capitalist and coordinator economies differ from their formal representations in ways that magnify their failings, while realistic participatory economies differ from their formal representation in ways that enhance their capacity to attain desirable results in fewer steps and at reduced cost.

6

FEASIBILITY

An important scientific innovation rarely makes its way by gradually winning over and converting its opponents: it rarely happens that Saul becomes Paul. What does happen is that its opponents gradually die out and that the growing generation is familiarized with the idea from the beginning.

—*Max Planck*

In chapter 1 we argued that efficiency, equity, self-management, solidarity, and variety were important goals that a desirable economy must attain. We also outlined why markets, central planning, private ownership of the means of production, hierarchical production relations, and inegalitarian consumption impede these goals. This left us no choice but to define new production, consumption, and allocation institutions to promote participatory, equitable outcomes.

In chapters 2, 3, and 4 we presented descriptions of new ways to organize production, consumption, and allocation and rebutted common criticisms. Finally, in chapter 5 we presented a continuous mathematical model of participatory planning and demonstrated that such a system could yield Pareto optimal outcomes under far less restrictive and more realistic assumptions than required to deduce efficiency properties for traditional economic models. In chapter 5 we also admitted that our mathematical model diverged in a number of regards from the more realistic descriptions of chapters 2 through 4 and investigated the implications of those divergences for the model's predictive powers. However, when we compared the differences between our mathematical model (FMPE) and our expectations for a realistic participatory economy (PE) with the differences between mathematical models of market and centrally planned economies and their well-known real world counterparts, we concluded that participatory economies are not only ideally *but also* practically superior to traditional market and centrally planned economies.

Nonetheless, there is one more step to make our argument complete. All theorists feel their theories are consistent and comprehensive. But often, of course, theorists are wrong. They present elegant, internally consistent arguments that seem accurate and comprehensive, but nonetheless lead to predictions at odds with reality. For example, we have argued elsewhere that traditional theorists have produced elegant and consistent but not so comprehensive and accurate arguments concerning the predictable attributes of capitalist and centrally planned economies.

So how can a theorist justify confidence in a set of theoretical results? What can others do to become more confident of our results or, alternatively, demonstrate their inadequacies? Of course it is possible to keep thinking about the results, reviewing the logic behind them, trying to discover inconsistencies or unwarranted assumptions. But it is also possible, at least in scientific disciplines, to conduct experiments. A good theoretical, scientific argument therefore includes indications of how to carry out experiments that might test predicted results.

So we need to specify some plausible, economic experiments. However, social environments are for obvious reasons notoriously hard to experiment with. The easiest "experiments" to implement are a variety of computer simulations in which various features of the system and assumptions about actors' behaviors can be altered to see how outcomes change. More problematic is implementing a whole "trial" participatory economy. While we feel there is little to lose from doing so, others might not share our low opinion of existing economies. But it is also possible to imagine establishing a kind of parallel participatory economy—or allocation system, in any event—alongside an existing market or centrally planned system. Without disrupting the functioning of the existing economy, differences between decisions reached via the two procedures could then be compared.

In this chapter we briefly describe a methodology for undertaking these "experiments." No new analyses or predictions regarding the behavior of participatory economic structures are presented and the material is chiefly for economists who want to undertake the experiments themselves. Since each of the "experiments" could usefully employ tools that actors in a real participatory economy would employ to keep track of proposals and results, and since describing these tools will also provide a review of how a real participatory economy should work, we start with this task.

Tracking a Participatory Economy

To generate a participatory plan, each consumer proposes the amount of each good she or he wishes to consume and the anticipated changes in her or his personal or material relations that will result. Each consumption unit proposes inputs and outputs equal to the sum of its members' proposals plus any collective goods or services desired. Larger consumption federations propose a summation of all member units' lists plus collective consumption.

Each production council chooses inputs and outputs including "technology," work hours, social relations, and labor intensities. Each industry sums its members' proposals. The whole economy's production is a summation of all its industries. From the production side there emerges a "net supply" of goods to meet a net "consumption demand" arising from consumer preferences.

Information Variables for a Participatory Economy

In chapter 5 we developed a mathematical formalism sufficient to demonstrate a series of propositions about a participatory economic model. We could arguably employ the same formalism for computer simulations that we would then use to determine the mean and variance of the number of iterations required to reach a feasible plan in a range of cases. Likewise, a variant of the mathematical formalism from the previous chapter might be usable for certain indicative calculations by actors in a real participatory economy. However, we indicated that there were some important differences between real participatory economics and its idealized model. Since we want any simulation we undertake to tell us about the realistic system and not our continuous mathematical model, we want the experiment's variables to be flexible enough to continually incorporate greater detail about the discrete behavior of a real system. Practically, we also want the simulation's variables to be suitable for programmers to incorporate as data types. And the same holds for a formalism that could be employed in a parallel participatory planning experiment within an existing economy. Here too, we do not want to use the kind of continuous variables that proved useful for technical proofs. Instead, we need a formalism suited for storage and retrieval of large amounts of discrete quantitative and qualitative data in an economy's computers, and useful to real producers and consumers who do not solve differential equations to make their decisions.

For all these reasons we begin by elaborating a new formalism suited to use in developing computer simulations and to continual refinement and enrichment in the course of experimentation.

We write the vector C^j, to represent consumer j's consumption input. To refer to consumption output, we write $\overline{C^j}$, where the bar tells us we are talking about outputs. Likewise, each production input vector will have entries corresponding to labor, machines, resources, and intermediate goods so P^j represents production inputs of unit j and $\overline{P^j}$ represents its outputs. In other words:

$$P^j = \left\{ P^j_1 \ldots P^j_k \ldots P^j_n \right\} \quad j = 1 \rightarrow \text{ProductionUnits}$$

$$\overline{P^j} = \left\{ \overline{P^j_1} \ldots \overline{P^j_k} \ldots \overline{P^j_n} \right\} \quad j = 1 \rightarrow \text{ProductionUnits}$$

$$C^j = \left\{ C^j_1 \ldots C^j_k \ldots C^j_n \right\} \quad j = 1 \rightarrow \text{Citizens}$$

$$\overline{C^j} = \left\{ \overline{C^j_1} \ldots \overline{C^j_k} \ldots \overline{C^j_n} \right\} \quad j = 1 \rightarrow \text{Citizens}$$

where n is the total number of *all* inputs and outputs.

Elaborating the new "language," a list is a sequence where each entry can be numbers, words, vectors, or even another list describing qualitative characteristics. For example, we could associate a special descriptive list with each workplace and with every input and output for every production and consumption actor. Vectors help actors assess quantities. Lists help actors assess qualities.

Finally, for every workplace there is a unit production matrix that, when multiplied by an input vector yields the unit's output vector. For convenience we can make all unit production matrices n by n, recognizing that many entries will be zero. Clearly, there is no technical impediment to communicating and manipulating information in these forms since computer techniques already allow efficient manipulation of vectors, matrices, and lists.

Manipulating Information

Each of our economy's industries has an input and output vector and a production matrix formed by aggregating the input and output vectors and production matrices of its members. Each consumer prepares a personal consumption input and output vector and list. Consumer units propose "summations" of their members' personal choices plus collective choices. This proceeds upward, until the whole economy has overall input and output consumption vectors summing all units' members' consumption plus all collective consumption.

For the first iteration, each worker proposes not only what she or he will contribute, but inputs and outputs for the whole plant. To get an indicative plant proposal out of all these worker proposals, we sum and then divide by the number of workers. This average is the best available estimate since at this stage no single viable plan better represents a summary of all workers' preferences. In later rounds input and output vectors for production units emerge directly as individuals no longer make separate proposals.

The industry matrix represents how all its units together act on input vectors. The societal matrix does the same for all industries composing the whole economy. Summing unit or industry production matrices involves taking a weighted average where the "weighing factor" is the relative volume of output in units. In a sense, each firm's production matrix is a "recipe" telling what ingredients will yield unit outputs of the "dinner" it is trying to prepare. By multiplying these "recipes" by any quantity of ingredients we can see what size meal will result. Alternatively, knowing the size of our dinner party, we can multiply the size meal we seek by the inverse of the production matrix to determine the ingredients needed. To sum the efforts of all the different cooks in all the different firms in an industry we simply add them together, taking account of the relative scale of operation of each to get an overall production matrix.

We already know that for the first two rounds, depending on iteration rules

$$P^{Plant(j)} = \frac{\sum_{i=1}^{NWP(j)} p_{ij}}{NWP(j)}$$

where $P^{Plant(j)}$ is the production input vector of the jth plant in the industry, NWP(j) is the number of workers in the plant, and p_{ij} is the ith worker's proposal for inputs for plant j.

For all subsequent rounds, units submit single proposals rather than proposals of each worker, and so for all rounds and the final plan

$$P^{Industry(k)} = \sum_{j=1}^{NPI(k)} P^{Plant(j)}$$

where $P^{Industry(k)}$ is the input vector for the kth industry in the economy and NPI(k) is the number of plants in industry k, and

$$P^E = \sum_{k=1}^{NIE} P^{Industry(k)}$$

where P^E is the input vector for the whole economy and NIE is just the number of industries in the economy, and, of course, similar results hold for outputs.

Considering the problem of summing lists, it would be inefficient to repeat a particular qualitative description just because each actor in a unit repeats it. Neither would it make sense to append conflicting statements in a growing jumble. Instead, if five consumers each have different qualitative descriptions under the entry referring to milk consumption, the unit's overall description should summarize all five in a short expression. Similarly, the same aggregating/summarizing process should occur for transition from units to neighborhood, neighborhood to ward, ward to county, and so on. We should remember, however, that all actors will have access not only to aggregated summary lists prepared by iteration facilitation boards, but to each unit's and individual's full formulation as well.

Functional Relationships

Suppose we look at values for a projected year. First we know that the unit, industry, or economy production input vector times the unit, industry, or economy production matrix will yield the unit, industry, or economy production output vector.

$$P^{Actor} \times [P^{Actor}] = \overline{P}^{Actor}$$

Second, for a plan to be feasible, the economy's production output vector must equal the total final consumption input vector plus the intermediate inputs of all the industries plus any planned slack.

$$\overline{P}^E = C^E + P^E + SL^E$$

The superscript "E" means that our vectors refer to the whole economy. SL^E is just our vector of all the [SL]ack pre-planned as a hedge against unforeseen changes in taste or productivity. Moreover, since equality of vectors only holds when each entry is equal, the above expression is shorthand for n equations, one for each vector entry. Here we can see that total supply for the economy is simply the output of the economy's production units. Total demand for the economy, on the other hand, is the sum of slack, production inputs, and consumer and consumer council inputs.

How does each unit and actor implement desires? What determines production matrices? What determines what the list of attributes of economic processes will be and how much each actor and collective unit will consume?

In assessing these and related questions, economists traditionally take consumer preferences, work force knowledge and skills, and technical options as independent variables determined outside the economy, and "derive" the values of what are called endogenous variables—inputs, outputs, and prices—under a particular institutional arrangment. Although this traditional approach is called a "general equilibrium" theory to emphasize that all factors mutually determine one another, in fact it treats certain factors as essentially determined outside the economy. In particular it ignores the fact that the institutional arrangements affect the "independent" variables, as we have pointed out. In contrast, while we recognize that extra-economic forces influence economic attributes, we make all economic institutions, norms, knowledge, preferences, prices, and quantities endogenous to the model.

Simulation Methodology

A simulation mimics how a participatory economy would operate under various assumptions about behavior and choices of planning rules. To use our "language" to track supply and demand in a simulation, we need iteration rules for economic behavior as well as working assumptions about how planning might affect people's tastes and behaviors.

For example, suppose one wants to test the hypothesis that some attribute, Z, necessarily characterizes participatory planning. One would need to demonstrate that the trajectory of development from first proposal to agreed plan to enacted plan necessarily enforces attribute Z under the full range of anticipated circumstances. Likewise, by using simulations one could investigate implications of changes in behavioral rules on outcomes. For example, one might study relations between the number of iterations allowed, the rules for each iteration, the speed with which actors settle on a plan, and the attributes the plan will have—over some range of assumed behaviors.

Alternatively, one could use simulations to research the effect of iteration workers on the plan's likely character, or the effect of planning collective consumption or industrial "investment" before rather than concurrently with personal consumption. Or we could compare the time it takes to go from random first round proposals to a settled plan, to the time it takes using first round proposals based closely on last year's final outcomes. Or we could test the effect of intransigence on the part of some range of participants. Or one could even try to determine under what behavioral assumptions a participatory economy would yield the same material outcomes that markets or central planning would produce.

But how would one actually undertake any of these studies? So far we have indicated only how to track part of what is going on. How can tracking hypothetical data facilitate analyses of what real economies would be like?

1. We need to track more variables, including prices, loans, and budgets.

2. We must determine how to simulate behavior in ways that realistically summarize consumers' and producers' diverse and altering preferences so we have something to track.

3. We must determine how to incorporate the effects of iteration rules.

This done, using behavioral assumptions and stipulating starting conditions, one could, with a sufficiently powerful computer and effective program, simulate a hypothetical economy to yield diverse insights about likely outcomes for different rules, behaviors, initial conditions, and so on.

Incorporating Prices and Budgets

Suppose we define every item, i, used in our economy (including labor) as having an indicative price π^i, so we can write a price vector $\pi = \{\pi_i\}$.

Any good or service embodies many other goods and services in its production, so that if we take one unit of any good or service "G,"

$$\pi(G) = \pi \times G$$

where G is a vector each of whose entries are the amount of the relevant item directly employed in producing one unit of G.

Suppose all society's actors settle on input and output vectors thereby establishing a plan. We can easily investigate the economy's techniques to determine and regularly update G for all goods so that once our planning process socially sets relations of production and inputs and outputs, indicative prices can be mechanically calculated by solving a system of linear equations. In short, social planning sets the relations between goods which in turn establish indicative prices, so that once we solve for these:

1. To find the socially valued worth of each consumption bundle we multiply the amounts of each good received by its price and sum.

2. To find the socially valued worth of the inputs and outputs of any plant, we multiply the amounts of these by their prices and sum.

Using V as a value operator to return "value" equal to a sum of prices times items

$$V[\,C^{Actor}\,] = \pi \times C^{Actor} = \sum_i \pi_i \times c_i^{\,Actor}$$

$$V[\,P^{Actor}\,] = \pi \times P^{Actor} = \sum_i \pi_i \times p_i^{\,Actor}$$

$$V[\,\overline{P}^{Actor}\,] = \pi \times \overline{P}^{Actor} = \sum_i \pi_i \times \overline{p}_i^{\,Actor}$$

We now easily define an actor's "loan" as the difference between the value of what the actor planned to receive and what the social average was after accounting for special circumstances that lead others to allow actors to go above or below average.

What about budgets? On the producer side, units assess their efforts and make proposals while respecting their projected industry per unit average output and their per resource productivity as guides to ensuring that their "social effectivity" is sufficient.

On the consumer side, each consumer ultimately settles on a bundle of consumption goods. The value of these, added to the per capita value of the consumer's public goods consumption, constitutes the total value of the consumer's consumption. Neglecting special excuses, loans, and/or debts, this must equal the societal average which serves, therefore, as a consumer budget.

What is the societal average consumption and therefore the budget constraint operating for each consumer? Clearly it is the value of total consumption for the economy divided by the total number of consumers.

$$B = \frac{\pi \times C^E}{N}$$

Simulation Actors

Consumers request goods and services in light of their needs and desires knowing that others will not approve unreasonable requests and that they will have to play an equitable role in producing whatever is to be consumed. Producers respond to consumer requests in light of their own needs and growing awareness of social circumstances. They balance their desires to work less and in more favorable circumstances against their own and other consumers' desires to consume more. How can we simulate the behavior of hundreds of millions of consumers and workers?

One simplification would be to use a scaled-down model including only a limited number of consumers and producers and a few intermediate and final goods. This approach would allow us to get a feel for the interaction at the micro scale. Another, more robust, option would be to truncate the choices of countless consumers into summary variables indicating total consumer demand for each of the available final consumer goods. This approach would give us better insight into the global trajectories of participatory planning. It also offers the option of establishing a kind of "game" format in which an individual, acting as a consumer or producer, interacts with the global simulation as one actor in the whole process.

To perform a small-scale simulation, we would let a few production units and consumption councils operate in the manner of real actors giving them hypothetical technologies and preferences and having a computer simulate their behavior as well as that of facilitation boards, and the like. In this way, tests with a given set of planning rules under different stipulations of technologies, preferences, and initial indicative prices would reveal how a particular system responds to different choices by the limited number of actors. Alternatively, one could keep the "economic environment" of technology and preferences constant and vary the planning rules to get an indication of the effects of different rule choices. The disadvantage of this kind of simulation is obviously that a real economy has tens of millions of participants, so that one might reasonably doubt that such simulation results are valid indicators of real results.

To pursue the more global approach requires some way of summarizing large numbers of producers' and consumers' behaviors. While the laws of probability and properties of the normal distribution can aid us considerably in doing this, there is a characteristic of production that requires a tactical compromise. In large-scale simulations we can incorporate differences in consumers' preferences by treating the demand for final goods as distributed normally around some mean. But differences in workers' preferences over work options cannot be treated so simply because factors other than their normally distributed personal preferences come into play in their choices, specifically, the special (and non-normally distributed) characteristics of production units. To do a simulation that tracks the behavior of every unit in each industry in the economy in light of its own particular characteristics would strain the capabilities of any available computer and no probabilistic shortcuts can fully circumvent this difficulty. But modeling industries rather than firms within industries is manageable, and using this approach we only lose details at the firm level, such as differences among firms due to unequal technologies. We of course still need a procedure to allow each industry to arrive at new proposals in each iteration, but we ought to be able to develop one in a way that acceptably approximates the range of possible outcomes that could arise from actually summing individual changes in each of the industry's firms. Thus, if we are content to simulate the behavior of industries rather than firms within industries, we can pursue large-scale simulation experiments as described below.

We require a way of simulating the sum of all producers' and consumers' behaviors so as to work with net supply and demand of industries on the one hand, and with net consumer demand for final consumption goods on the other. Ideally, the simulation would help identify the bounds that behavior would have to fall within for the system to operate desirably under some range of planning rules. So can we really expect to sensibly go from hundreds of millions of consumers or millions of consumers' councils to total consumer demand for each good without incorporating any individual choices?

The task is similar to trying to simulate the behavior of gases in enclosed containers. No one can track the positions and velocities of all the molecules. Even with a supercomputer, this micro approach would be fruitless. But if we ask what proportion of the molecules will be where with this or that velocity we can understand and simulate important macro properties like pressure and temperature without confronting the behavior of each individual gas molecule.

Analogously, in studying hypothetical participatory economies we cannot possibly simulate the individual choices of millions of individual production units and hundreds of millions of individual consumers. For production units, as noted above, we forgo details of individual units and track industry behavior instead. What about consumption?

The obvious choice is to pay attention only to consumers' councils or federations. Better still is to track only total demand for each final good. The idea is to deduce qualities of the trajectory of collective behavior in light of iteration rules, the size of the economy, and plausible assumptions about the range of consumers' behaviors and how these sum to total supply and demand. Regarding consumption, to assess total demand we only need to know that some number of people will choose one thing, and another number of people will choose another, ignoring who will choose what. By bypassing each individual's particular behaviors we only lose information regarding the exigencies of individual interaction with the system. Does the individual get bogged down, inevitably become irritated? Does the size of consumer units play a role in the rate of the whole process? Do geographic distributions matter? Some of these possibilities can be assessed, however, by constructing a means for a real individual or group of individuals to join in the simulation process at a real time terminal connected with the unfolding simulation.

Returning to the general problem of summarizing total consumption without incorporating individual actor's behaviors, we can reasonably assume that consumers' preferences will form a normal curve whose main characteristics are completely determined by two parameters, mean and standard deviation, where the maximum number of respondents always occurs at the mean and varies directly with the total number of respondents and inversely with the standard deviation. Knowing these gross attributes can so simplify the simulation that we can do it for any number of hypothetical consumers.

Suppose we track the milk totals all citizens request in the first iteration of a year's plan. We can say nothing definitive about any one person's choice but we can plausibly assume that the distribution of the choices of all actors will fall on a normal curve. If we assume this is true for all goods, plausible conclusions can be reached. But even this hypothesis could be checked by also undertaking simulations assuming other probability distributions.

Incorporating Actual Behavior

Having settled on industries and the whole population of consumers as our unit actors, from iteration to iteration, for each good the simulation must incorporate algorithms for generating new indicators for total supply (production output) and total demand (production input plus consumer demand plus slack) in light of assumptions about the interaction between consumer and producer behavior, the prior status of each good, available qualitative information, and the like. One can then program the simulation to calculate product status for each new iteration up to the final plan.

To get total supply in each iteration we will need to incorporate a rule for how each industry goes from one proposal to the next in light of possible iteration rules, the prior status of each good, and the producers' preferences for work versus leisure. A sensible rule would include a component for moving toward (or away) from the prior iteration's consumer demand (or the iteration-board projected consumer demand for the current iteration) plus a component for moving toward or away from the prior iteration's (or the current projected) total production requirement (averaged over units). To build in a spectrum of unpredictability reflecting diverse and changing producer preferences as well as the effect of diverse iteration rules that would appear in a real society, we can imagine programming into our algorithm a degree of weighted random choice that would be correlated with supply and demand conditions and with allocation rules. In this way we can reasonably test for a whole range of conceivable industry preferences.

For example, we might employ a rule that for any industry the proposal in a current iteration will reduce the discrepancy between supply and demand in the prior iteration for the industry's good by a random multiplier between -.25 (which would increase by 25% of the discrepancy) and .5 (which would reduce by 50% of the discrepancy) with a bias introduced by always adding some particular fraction, say δG, to the random number picked by the computer where the range of δG would increase or decrease in tune with supply and demand conditions, iteration rules, some attribute of the particular industry, and so on. We could then test for the effect of different definitions of δG reflecting different possible producer response characteristics as well as different initial ranges of proposal alterations. To refine the system still further, we could put in proportionality factors to account for the different values of the output of different industries thereby keeping the drift in industry proposals from one iteration to the next within some range regarding their impact on overall consumption budgets. Naturally, as a byproduct of dealing with producer proposals for output we automatically handle producer inputs as these are directly calculable from outputs by way of production matrices and, in this light, a further refinement in the algorithm would incorporate attention to the impact of under- or over-supply of its own input components in each unit's tendency to decrease or increase its production proposal. It should be clear that while we have not explicitly incorporated production preference functions for individual workers, we have indicated a means to simulate the full range of conceivable behavior patterns that possible workplace characteristics and workers' preferences could induce.

This said, however, we still have the problem of simulating consumer demand. First we can plot any consumer demand distribution to generate a list of ordered pairs, (x,y) where the x-entry is a desired amount that a consumer could propose as her or his demand, and the y-entry is the total number of consumers proposing that amount. In this light we can usefully write consumer demand distributions for a particular good in a particular iteration, I, as $C^I(G)$, where this operator returns lists of ordered pairs. The "I" superscript will take on (1) the number value of the iteration if we are talking about an iteration distribution, (2) the value "p" if we are talking about the plan agreed to by the planning process, or (3) the value "f" if we are talking about the year's [f]inal outcomes as they are actually enacted.

In a real economy we would of course get our ordered pairs for any iteration's consumer demand distribution from summing all the participatory planning consumer input vectors, thereby incorporating precise actor by actor information. Yet, in our global simulation, even without knowing or predicting every consumer's own unique input vector, we can still simulate total consumer demand for each good by using distributions to represent gross characteristics of taste, much as we used a statistical range of production iteration choices with flexible parameters and built-in biases to simulate the effects of diverse producer preferences and plant characteristics on industry production proposals. We therefore skip the enumeration of vectors for every actor and instead jump directly to approximate expressions for the entire ensemble of actors.

Define for any consumer demand distribution for iteration "I" the total demand for the good G, $D(G)$, to equal the sum of the number of people demanding a certain amount of G times the amount for all such ordered pairs in that consumer demand distribution.

$$D(G) = Tot\,[C^{I}(G)] \;=\; \sum_{i} x_i \times y_i \quad \text{for all } (x_i, y_i) \text{ in } C^{I}(G)$$

Tot operates on a consumer demand distribution for any good to give the total demand for that good. Each of the terms added is just the number of actors times the amount they want to consume. We can now define [ST]atus of the good G in the iteration I as the difference between the total supply offered and the total demand and slack desired for that good in that iteration. Tot and ST are operators that return numbers, not vectors or lists. Remembering that total supply is just production output and total demand is consumer demand plus producer input demand plus slack:

$$ST^{I}(G) = \overline{P}^{E}(G)^{I} - P^{E}(G)^{I} - D^{I}(G) - SL^{I}(G)$$

If we define the net supply of any good G, $S^{I}(G)$, as the total producer output of G minus the total producer input of G, or the amount of G coming from production and available for slack or consumer demand, we can write the simpler equation:

$$ST^{I}(G) = S^{I}(G) - D^{I}(G) - SL^{I}(G)$$

Given all this, and assuming that it can converge, the participatory planning process can be summarized in the following succinct fashion. For any good G, the net supply distribution follows the trajectory

$$S^1(G) \rightarrow S^2(G) \rightarrow S^3(G) \rightarrow S^4(G) \rightarrow S^5(G) \rightarrow S^i(G)$$

and likewise for demand, slack, and status distributions with suitable changes in notation.

The problem is to discern what range of planning rules and what types of consumer and producer behavior will allow the status trajectory of each good to move toward zero in an acceptable number of iterations.

Within our simulation methodology we have already indicated the main ideas for establishing algorithms for arriving at each new iteration's producer inputs and outputs for any G given the prior iteration's results. This establishes net supply. Since slack is socially chosen, its level is at the disposal of the simulator. Only consumer demand remains.

In each iteration all consumers receive a facilitation board projection for total societal and average per capita consumption of each good and for estimated average consumption bundles and unit by unit production averages. Since we know how to track these variables, what we need to know to describe the macro-trajectory of our economy's net supply, its consumer demand distributions, and its slack requirements from iteration to iteration until the model settles on a plan, is how to characterize the effects of preferences, planning rules, current divergences, and choices about budget levels on changes in consumption distributions from iteration to iteration.

Consumer Demand

Parameters distinguishing any particular economy depend on the economy's number of actors, number of products, number and structure of industries, and technologies.

The first iteration proposals presented by all producers and consumers sum to determine net supply and total consumer demand proposals which, coupled with preferences about slack, determine status relations for each good. Since in our modeling we bypass individual preferences, the aim of our earlier discussions of individual behavior was to: (1) reveal the underlying dynamics of macro relations, (2) demonstrate a notation to allow facilitation board manipulations and public reporting in a real economy, and (3) further clarify the source of indicative prices.

Now, however, to pursue a macro approach we must focus on consumer distributions and the changing statuses of simulated goods, not on individual actor's activities.

We start by assuming that for every good, G, there is a first round consumer demand distribution $C^1(G)$ characterized by a mean, $\mu\{C^1(G)\}$, and standard deviation, $\sigma\{C^1(G)\}$, for each good.

We also write for any good that its distribution's facilitation board projected average for an iteration—just the average amount demanded per consumer—is $Proj[C^I(G)]$ and similarly for net supply. We also define $\delta\{C^I(G)\}$ and $\delta\{S^I(G)\}$ to be the "proportionality factor" between the real mean of the demand and the net supply of good G and their before-the-fact projected averages.

$$Proj\,[C^I(G)]\,[1 + \delta\{C^I(G)\}] = \mu\{C^I(G)\}$$

So that, if

$$\delta\{C^I(G)\} > 0$$

the projected average is less than the actual registered average and if

$$\delta\{C^I(G)\} < 0$$

the projected average is more than the actual registered average.

And, likewise

$$Proj\,[S^I(G)]\,\{1 - \delta\,S^I(G)\} = \mu\{S^I(G)\}$$

So that if

$$\delta\{S^I(G)\} > 0$$

the projected average is more than the actual registered average and if

$$\delta\{S^I(G)\} < 0$$

the projected average is less than the actual registered average.

Then, extending and simplifying this notation, the hypothetical average consumer requests a total amount of any good $(1+\delta C) \times$ (the projected average demand for that good), formulated with a plus sign to reflect the likelihood that the average consumer will have a higher estimate of economic growth than facilitation workers. Likewise, the average producer proposes to supply a total amount of any good $(1-\delta S) \times$ (the projected average supply for that good), reflecting the likelihood of producer optimism.

It is important at this point to note that while unique indicative prices are calculable for any balanced plan, no such prices are calculable for early iteration proposals that are not yet balanced. To use our value function during iterations we must use prices that derive indirectly from facilitation board workers' updated estimates of likely final plans. Although this is no problem in participatory practice, it is not easily implemented in a simulation lacking facilitation workers and having only hypothetical "generic" actors. We can, however, do the next best thing and use last year's indicative prices during the first iteration, and then, for subsequent iterations, use a simple algorithm to decide how to correct the median of the proposed total demand and proposed total supply for each good to attain overall balance of all inputs and outputs as if the results were facilitation board generated amounts acceptable for calculating indicative prices via production matrices. A real world system can then do at least as well as our simulation by using this mechanical procedure to calculate indicative prices. It could likely do better using more sophisticated algorithms or relying on actual facilitation workers. Given these elaborate steps, there emerge a number of equations that can help us understand our system.

First, for any normal distribution, the mean times the total number of actors is equal to what we call the "Tot" of the distribution. If we use this relation to consider the demand distribution for a particular good, G, we find

$$Tot\left[C^I(G)\right] = \sum_i x_i \times y_i = \mu\left\{C^I(G)\right\} N$$

where $N = \sum_i y_i$ is just the total number of consumers.

Temporarily ignoring slack, the value of all goods of type G demanded in any iteration will be

$$Val\,[\,Tot\,[C^I(G)]\,] = Val\,[\,\mu\left\{C^I(G)\right\}\,]\,N = \pi^G\,[\,\mu\left\{C^I(G)\right\}\,]\,N$$

Likewise, the value of the total net supply of all goods of type G is given by

$$Val\,[\,Tot\,[S^I(G)]\,] = Val\,[\,\mu\{S^I(G)\,]\,N = \pi^G\left\{\mu\,S^I(G)\right\}N$$

Similarly, the value of all goods of all types demanded will be

$$\sum_G Val\,[Tot\,[C^I(G)]] = \sum_G Val\,[\,\mu C^I(G)\,]\,N = \sum_G [\,\pi^G\mu\left\{C^I(G)\right\}N$$

So, if we write

$$\hat{\mu}(D)$$

as the vector of all the demand means and

$$\hat{\mu}(S)$$

as the vector of all the supply means, then we have for the value of all goods demanded

$$\sum_G Val\,[Tot\,[C^I(G)]] = \pi\times\hat{\mu}(D)\,]\,N$$

And for the value of all goods supplied for consumption

$$\sum_G Val\,[Tot\,[S^I(G)]] = \pi\times\hat{\mu}(S)\,]\,N$$

At this point we can also write the value of total producer demand as

$$Val\,[P^{\,Economy}] = \pi\times P^{\,Economy}$$

If we assume that for each good we want our slack to be some fixed percentage of the total net supply of that good, say, for the sake of this discussion, 5 percent, we can write

$$ST^I(G) = Tot\,[S^{\,I}(G)] - Tot\,[C^I(G)] - Tot\,[SL^{\,I}(G)]$$

as

$$ST^I(G) = Tot\,[S^I(G)] - .95Tot\,[C^I(G)\,]$$

And then

$$ST^I(G) = N\,[\hat{\mu}(S) - .95\hat{\mu}(D)\,]$$

It ought to be evident from all this that by using these and related expressions, facilitation workers could track and chart many relationships that citizens could examine to help them make their choices. But our primary concern here is tracking what the economy will likely do over the whole planning period and, as a result, the next step is not to delve into how individual actors might use various types of information to make their decisions, but instead to determine how groups of people will respond to iterations so that we can go from $C^1[G]$ to $C^i[G]$ one step at a time. The most general way to approach this problem is to use the same technique we used with initial consumer response.

Each iteration has its own rules. We assume each iteration will be characterized by some average most probable and frequent behavior so that everyone's behavior will form a distribution characterized by this average as mean and by some particular standard deviation that will vary from good to good.

Suppose we had some rule for a particular iteration constraining the ways actors can alter their prior proposal. Then all the people who had previously said they wanted 300 pints of milk will now re-choose for all goods, including milk, moving up and down in their requests however they decide within the rule constraint. In particular, if we think in terms of a round's distribution of milk demand encompassing the array of ordered pairs (x_i, y_i), then all the people, y_i, who wanted any particular value x_i in any particular round will constitute a new group in the following round.

Moreover, each of these new groups will respond to the need to make a new milk proposal from a position of having the same prior milk proposal (though different proposals for other goods) and of confronting the same iteration rules. They will not all do the same thing, of course, but, assuming these groups are large, it is plausible to assume that in going from one iteration to another all the members of a new group will alter their proposals so their new choices will together form a new distribution whose mean is shifted away from their prior proposal for the good by an amount that depends on the rules of the iteration, the projected price for the good, the prior round's status for the good, and the ratio of the prior round's "x_i" to the prior round's mean for the good (how far out on the normal curve the group is). The new distribution for all actors' choices for any good, G, will be the sum of the new component distributions for that good and will have a clear relation to the prior distribution which we can deduce in terms of our various distribution functions and relations.

In short, given demand or supply distributions for a good and workable assumptions about behavioral responses to iterative rules in light of anticipated budget constraints, we can create an algorithm able to derive subsequent distributions for later iterations.

For example, assume we have the demand distribution for iteration I for some good G, $C^I[G]$. Any consumers who have requested the same quantity of good "G" in round I will constitute a new group for purposes of round I+1.

Moreover, each of these new groups will make choices that will fall on a new distribution curve. The new mean for each group will be moved from the value of the group's prior choice by an amount depending on the good's prior status, the budget, the iteration rule, and the divergence of the group's prior choice from the prior mean for the good. The new standard deviation will be some new value also depending on iteration rules, the good, and the group.

Now, if we let $\delta\mu$ stand for the difference between the mean recorded for iteration I+1 and the starting value set in iteration I, the result is that if n people were previously requesting the same amount of a good G in iteration I, in iteration I+1 those n people would be requesting a range of amounts forming a normal curve with mean equal to the prior round's mean plus the change $\delta\mu$. The only conceptual difficulty is characterizing $\delta\mu$ in terms of relevant factors in a realistic fashion. Having done so, it is merely mathematical manipulation to use the knowledge of how each subgroup of actors might change their choices to determine what will be the change in the overall demand. Moreover, to cover all plausible trajectories at this step we can investigate a range of parametized algorithms.

Given this approach to determining $C^2(G)$ given knowledge of $C^1(G)$ and the other relevant factors influencing the process, then coupled with our earlier results it becomes possible to track any participatory planning system from first proposal to settled plan in light of whatever choices of rules for each iteration and behavioral assumptions for actors we might wish to consider. This gives us the capability of determining under what conditions and rules outcomes are optimal, acceptable, or unacceptable.

Since all these approaches would work at the level of distributions for the preferences *of the entire population* and therefore fail to reveal much about the *iteration to iteration circumstances of individuals*, an additional step might be employed to give feedback about this micro level.

One option, as noted earlier, is to examine a vastly simplified instance in detail by simulating an economy with a limited number of consumers and producers including tracking each individual actor's choices in detail.

A second and more interesting option, however, is to incorporate an individual or a group of individuals into the macro simulation. The individual, or group, would participate in each iteration round at a terminal using data from the whole simulation in the same way that a real actor would use data from the whole rest of a participatory economy. The individual's (or group's) choices would then become part of the data for the new iteration, and so on, to conclusion. This would help clarify the exigencies of individual interaction in participatory planning.

Experiment 2: Developing a Parallel Economy

A simulation incorporates more detail than a differential economic model, but still misses the richness of living interaction. As a result, the full characteristics of participatory economics and the diverse solutions to institutional problems associated with it will ultimately only reveal themselves in actual operations. We will not even know many of the most interesting questions that practitioners might ask until we enact a real participatory economic system. While working to accomplish a revolutionary transformation of existing economies, can any lesser activity intimate more revealingly than a simulation what would happen?

Conceivably one could run a "shadow" participatory economy within an existing economy. This could occur in a subset of the whole economy, whether geographic or by industrial sector, and could be carried out at the level of individuals or groups. Its operations could be evaluated in themselves and also compared to results in the real existing economy. Although this type experiment could be carried out anywhere, it is easiest to imagine in a centrally planned economy with a serious interest in progressive experimentation. In the best scenario, the experiment might expand from one sector to the whole economy and not only serve as a laboratory to test participatory planning, but also as a school, both educating the public and developing the means to implement participatory planning without undue disruption.

What is most important to emphasize regarding this now completed chapter, however, is that the formalism employed here could not only be employed to develop computer simulations, but also improved for use by iteration workers, producers, consumers, and programmers in actual participatory economies or participatory economic experiments.

CONCLUSION

I am an invisible man.... I am a man of substance, of flesh and bone, fiber and liquids—and I might even be said to possess a mind. I am invisible, understand, simply because people refuse to see me.

—Ralph Ellison

If we do not now dare everything, the fulfillment of that prophecy, re-created from the Bible in song by a slave, is upon us: God gave Noah the rainbow sign. No more water, the fire next time!

—James Baldwin

In chapter 1, we explained why traditional economic solutions are incompatible with participation and equity. More specifically we explained why private enterprise, hierarchical production and consumption, and markets and central planning subvert self-management and solidarity and bias the conditions of economic choice in ways that lead to increasing inefficiencies.

So a participatory, egalitarian economy must consist of nonhierarchical production and consumption relations and nonmarket, noncentral planning allocation.

Following this injunction, in chapters 2 and 3 we described procedures for making production and consumption participatory and equitable. We explained the importance of democratic councils, balanced work complexes, and participatory workplace and consumption decision making, noting the information that allocation procedures would have to provide to make these institutions viable. Specifically, we argued that participatory economics requires:

1. Councils that foster economic democracy within each workplace and consumption unit.

2. Balanced work complexes and egalitarian consumption opportunities.

3. Workplace and consumption decision making norms emphasizing the well-being of producers and consumers alike and promoting solidarity.

And we argued that none of this was incompatible with an efficient use of productive potentials or with incentives needed to elicit effort.

In chapter 4 we described participatory allocation including iterative bargaining, rules for converging, procedures for updating plans, facilitation boards, and how the "communicative tools" of prices, measures of work, and qualitative information would be utilized. In chapter 5 we demonstrated that a formal model of our participatory economy converges to an efficient plan under far less stringent and more realistic assumptions than traditional alternatives. We also explained why realistic versions of participatory planning could be expected to better approximate the performance of its formal model than realistic versions of market or central planning approximate the performance of their formal models.

This allowed us to argue the superiority of participatory economics, subject to concerns about the viability of its practical implementation. Finally, in chapter 6 we presented a methodology for simulation and policy "experiments" that might further substantiate our claim that participatory economics is a viable as well as desirable economic option.

We believe we have made a *prima facie* case for further examining a participatory vision. For those who would like to live in a better world, the implications seem clear. Quoting Noam Chomsky, "The task for a modern industrial society is to achieve what is now technically realizable, namely, a society which is really based on free voluntary participation of people who produce and create, live their lives freely within institutions they control and with limited hierarchical structures, possibly none at all."